Some Hard Questions

CHRIS WRIGHT

OXFORD

OXFORD
UNIVERSITY PRESS

Great Clarendon Street, Oxford OX2 6DP

Oxford University Press is a department of the University of Oxford. It furthers the University's objective of excellence in research, scholarship, and education by publishing worldwide in

Oxford New York

Auckland Bangkok Buenos Aires Cape Town Chennai Dar es Salaam Delhi Hong Kong Istanbul Karachi Kolkata Kuala Lumpur Madrid Melbourne Mexico City Mumbai Nairobi São Paulo Shanghai Singapore Taipei Tokyo Toronto

with an associated company in Berlin

Database right Oxford University Press (maker)

First published 2002

British Library Cataloguing in Publication Data

Data available

ISBN 0 19 914805 8

10 9 8 7 6 5 4 3 2

Typesetting and design: Carole Binding, Ruth Nason

Illustrations: John Haslam

Printed in Spain by Edelvives, Zaragoza

The Author and Publisher are grateful to the following for helpful comments at various times during the preparation of the book:

Leon Bernstein, Mark Brimicombe, Rasamandala Das, Roy Ahmad Jackson, Venerable Kusalo, Chris Prescott, Kanwaljit Kaur Singh, Jos Sumner

Cover photo: A grief-stricken woman, whose village had been destroyed by an earthquake (Corbis Images/David and Peter Turnley).

Introduction

We live in a world where there are people of many different religions. In many of our towns and cities Buddhists, Christians, and Hindus live alongside Muslims, Jews, and Sikhs. If you travel abroad, you will soon experience whole countries that have been shaped by religion.

The *Religion for Today* series gives you the skills and knowledge to understand people with beliefs different from your own. In learning about other religions you will also have the chance to think about your own life. So you will not only learn *about* the religions you study; you will also learn *from* the religions.

Each book is packed with sources. Some are quotations from the sacred books of the religions. Others come from people who practise the religions. As you read each source you need to ask yourself: Who wrote it? Why did they write it? What sort of writing is it? Is the source reliable? Is it authoritative? Is it biased or one-sided? Do you agree with what is being said in the source? Do sources in the same unit contradict each other?

This book, *Some Hard Questions*, encourages you to explore some of the big questions in life, such as: How do we know God exists?, How did the universe begin?, Why do people suffer?, and Where do we go when we die? You will learn how religions attempt to answer these questions.

Contents

Learning about religion

More than three-quarters of the world's population consider that they belong to a religion. But what is religion? In Unit 1.1 we will explore what religion and being religious mean. There are many different religions around the world and you will meet ideas from several of them in this book. Unit 1.2 introduces the main religions that we will study. Unit 1.3 looks at the value of learning about religion.

1.1

What is religion?

1 What do you think a 'religious' person is? How does such a person stand out? What qualities should they have?

2 Would you say that you are a religious person? What makes you religious or not?

3 Do you think that religion has any effect on the world?

The majority of people say that they are religious. In a crowd, do you think you can pick out who is religious? Do you think people show that they are religious, or not, in their everyday life?

Being religious means many different things to different people. We are going to explore what religion is actually about. Examples from some religions are given to illustrate the different points. But many more examples from other religions could have been chosen for each point. The world's religions share many of the same broad features.

Religions are about:

● **searching for Truth or God**
   Many people feel that there is something beyond everyday human life, which explains the way things are. They try to find or understand what that 'something' is. In some religions, God is believed to be guiding the world, as its creator. In other religions, there is an Ultimate Truth.

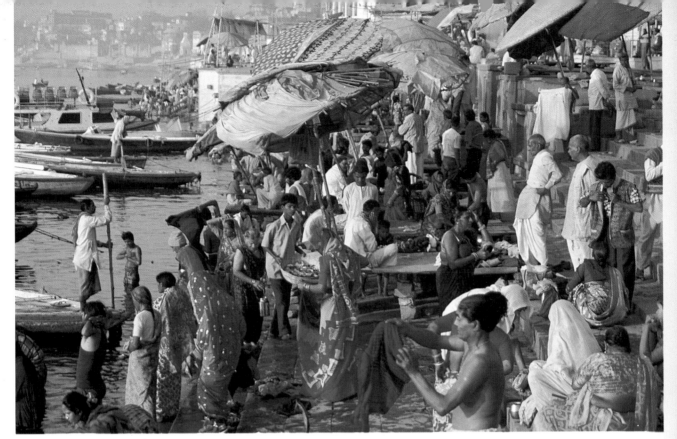

● **holding certain beliefs and following certain teachings**

- Most religions have a belief in God, although they differ in what they think about God.

- Most religions give guidance on how to lead your life.

- Most religions help to answer hard questions such as: How did the world begin?, Why is there suffering?, and What happens after death?

Many people, like these Hindus at Varanasi, go on pilgrimage – a journey to a place that is sacred in their religion. The physical journey mirrors an inward spiritual journey to come closer to God or the Ultimate Truth.

● **following certain practices**
Religions may have rules or customs about clothing, food, and other everyday matters, as well as about ways of worshipping and praying.

➤ *For Muslims, praying five times a day is one of five basic practices called 'the Pillars of Islam'.*

● worshipping together in special buildings

In most religions, people gather together regularly to worship God. They have special buildings where worship takes place.

4 People worship in many different ways. How can you tell that the activities in the photographs on this page are religious? What do they have in common? How do they differ?

◀ *Worshipping God is an important part of Christian everyday life. Many Christians gather together on Sundays to worship in churches.*

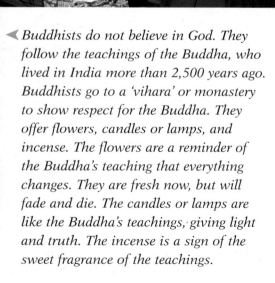

◀ *Buddhists do not believe in God. They follow the teachings of the Buddha, who lived in India more than 2,500 years ago. Buddhists go to a 'vihara' or monastery to show respect for the Buddha. They offer flowers, candles or lamps, and incense. The flowers are a reminder of the Buddha's teaching that everything changes. They are fresh now, but will fade and die. The candles or lamps are like the Buddha's teachings, giving light and truth. The incense is a sign of the sweet fragrance of the teachings.*

- **reading texts called scriptures**
  Scriptures teach people beliefs and values. Some scriptures are believed to be words from God, and so people try to obey these scriptures in their lives.

- **sharing important moments of life**
  There are events in life that people don't want to experience alone – joyous moments such as birth and marriage, and sad times such as the death of a loved one. Religions have special ceremonies for these times in people's lives. The ceremonies enable people to share important experiences and to support each other.

▲ *Sikhs meet to worship in a building called a gurdwara. Afterwards, everyone stays to share a meal called 'langar'. This shows the Sikh belief that all people are equal members of God's human family.*

◄ *Jewish teaching says that a boy is an adult at the age of 13. He is then called Bar Mitzvah, which means 'Son of the Commandment'. At his Bar Mitzvah ceremony the boy reads from the Torah, the most important part of the Jewish Bible.*

● **belonging to a community**

A religious community can mean all the people who go to worship at a local church, mosque, synagogue, or other religious building. It can also mean everyone around the world who belongs to a particular religion – for example, the Sikh community. Both these types of community have people in charge, who teach and guide others in their religion. This protects the religion's beliefs and teachings. In some religions people try to persuade more people to join their community. Getting someone to take on the beliefs of a religion is called converting them.

▼ *Our beliefs and values affect the way we see the world.*

● **expressing beliefs and values in social action**

What people believe affects the way they view the world and the way they live their lives. Religions shape people's beliefs about where the world and humans have come from, the purpose of life, what happens after death, and how to behave towards others. Many people believe it is important to put others' needs before their own. This belief leads some people to do charity work or to stand up for human rights.

▼ *Religious beliefs lead some people to use their skills to help the needy. Here a volunteer doctor treats street children in Guatemala.*

5 Choose two pictures in Unit 1.1. Imagine that you took the pictures, in order to show 'what religion is about'. Explain what each picture shows and what it says about being religious.

A religious world

The main religions followed by people in Great Britain are Buddhism, Christianity, Hinduism, Islam, Judaism, and Sikhism. The map shows the spread of these religions across the world. They can be grouped into two 'families'. One has its roots in India, and consists of Hinduism, Buddhism, and Sikhism. The other has its roots in the Middle East, and consists of Judaism, Christianity, and Islam. The religions in each family have certain things in common.

▼ *This map gives a simplified picture of religions around the world. It shows only which religion is followed by most people in each country. In fact, many countries including Great Britain have followers of more than one religion.*

1 a Which continent has the largest distribution of Hindus?

   b Which continents have the largest spread of Muslims?

   c What do you notice about the spread of Christianity?

   d Write your own title and caption for the map, explaining what it tells you.

■ Hinduism	■ Islam
▨ Buddhism	■ Chinese
▨ Sikhism	■ Tribal
■ Judaism	▨ Tribal/Christianity
■ Christianity	▨ Tribal/Christianity/Islam

Hinduism has no founder. The origins of the religion are traced to a great civilisation living in the Indus Valley.

The origins of Judaism are traced to Abraham, 'father of the Jews', about 2000 BCE.

Jews measure time from creation. This makes 2002 CE the Jewish year 5763.

Buddhism began when Siddattha Gotama became enlightened. He was born in 563 BCE in Lumbini, near the modern border between India and Nepal.

2000BCE

563 BCE

The Timeline above shows when and how our six religions began. Today, they all have millions of followers.

The number of followers in each religion

	Number	Percentage of world population
Buddhism	314,939,000	5.7
Christianity	1,833,022,000	33.4
Hinduism	732,812,000	13.4
Islam	971,328,700	17.7
Judaism	17,822,000	0.3
Sikhism	18,800,500	0.3

In history books dates are often described as BC or AD. This way of dating, which is used internationally, was based on Christian beliefs about Jesus Christ. BC stands for 'before Christ'. AD (Anno Domini) means 'in the year of Our Lord'. AD dates are counted from the year in which Christians believe that Jesus was born. Nowadays, the initials BCE (Before the Common Era) and CE (Common Era) are often used instead of BC and AD. This shows respect for other religions, which count the years of their history from different starting points.

2 **a** Using the figures above, draw a pie chart to represent the numerical spread of the religions in the world.

b What do these figures tell you? Which religions have the most followers? Does this mean that these religions are the strongest? What does 'strong' mean?

c What are the difficulties of figures like these? How do you think they were collected? How did the people collecting the figures know which religion people followed?

d Should religions try to convert people, to get more followers?

Christianity started as people followed the teachings of Jesus. He was born into a Jewish family in present-day Israel in about 6 BCE. His followers believed he was the Son of God.

Muslims say that their religion, Islam, is as old as humanity but that the Prophet Muhammad started the Islamic community in Arabia in 622 CE.

Sikhism was founded in 1499 by Guru Nanak, in the Punjab region of northern India.

0   33CE   622 CE   1499 CE

Over time, religions have spread from their places of origin as people moved and introduced their religion to other countries. For example, Christianity has spread all over the world. As people in different places became Christians, they still kept their own customs and some of the traditions of their old religions. This means that, around the world, Christianity is expressed in many different ways.

▲ *Christians on All Souls' Day in Poland (above) and*
◄ *India (left). On All Souls' Day, every 2 November, Roman Catholic Christians pray for the souls of people who have died. They believe that the souls are in Purgatory, a place where they suffer for their sins before they can go to heaven.*

Both Christianity and Islam have spread in Africa, and the religious nature of the continent has changed. The maps in the top row show how the percentage of the population following African tribal religions went down in different African countries, during the twentieth century.

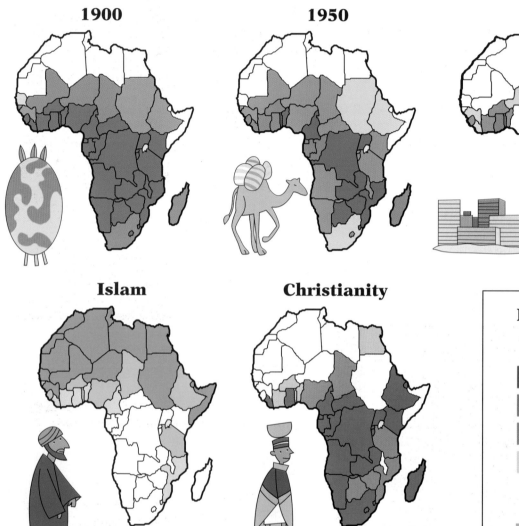

1900   **1950**   **1990**

Islam   **Christianity**

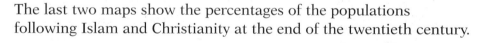

The last two maps show the percentages of the populations following Islam and Christianity at the end of the twentieth century.

Key

- 70%
- 50%
- 30%
- 10%

- 50%
- 30%
- 10%

- 50%
- 30%
- 10%

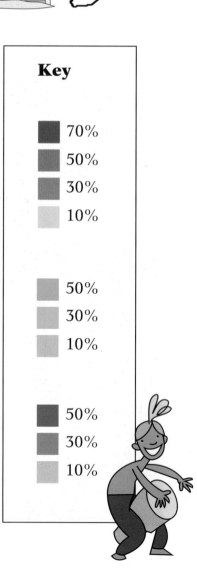

3   What can you learn from these maps about the way in which the religious nature of Africa has changed in the last hundred years? Can you suggest any reasons for this change?

4   **a** What does the information in Unit 1.2 tell you about the place of religion in the world?

b After looking at this information, what questions do you need to ask? What does Unit 1.2 *not* tell you?

1.3

Why learn about religion?

People's religious beliefs and background influence the way they think, the way they view the world, the things they do, and the way they live their lives. This makes religion a powerful force in society. The pictures on pages 13 and 14 show some examples. Knowing about different religions can help you to understand people's actions and ideas. It can also help you understand some of the things that happen in the world.

➤ *Religious belief motivates people to help others, even in situations where they may be putting themselves in danger. This international aid worker helped refugees fleeing from violence in Rwanda.*

◀ *Archbishop Desmond Tutu and Bishop Trevor Huddleston were active campaigners against the apartheid system in South Africa. Here they expressed their joy that apartheid had ended.*

source A

One reason why Desmond Tutu became a Christian priest was to fight the injustice of South Africa's apartheid system, which separated blacks from whites. His beliefs about justice and his hatred of discrimination come from his religious book, the Bible. He says:

'The Bible is the most revolutionary, the most radical book there is ... When God encounters injustice, oppression, exploitation, he takes sides ... he is a God of surprises, uprooting the powerful and the unjust to establish his kingdom.'

from S. du Boulay, *Voice of the Voiceless* (1988)

Religion often appears in news stories. In September 2000 Jewish, Christian, and Buddhist leaders took part in a march for peace. They were attending a conference of political and religious leaders to discuss ways for peace in the world.

1 **a** Look through some recent newspapers, either in the library or on the internet. Pick out any stories that mention religion. Cut out or print out the stories and collect them on an RE News board. Underneath each story write two or three lines saying what is the main issue in the story.

b Write a few sentences explaining how Religious Education can help you understand the world in which you live.

Religious beliefs have often led to conflict. This is particularly so in Israel, where Jews, Muslims, and Christians all have important religious sites. This Palestinian guard holds prayer beads while on duty.

In 2001 Buddhist monks protested when ancient statues of the Buddha in Afghanistan were destroyed by the Taliban, the Islamic rulers of the country.

Arguments for RE

As well as helping you to understand events, learning about religion enables you to appreciate music and art that have been influenced by religious ideas. Also it gives you the opportunity to think about what *you* believe and do not believe – both with regard to moral issues and in response to the 'hard questions' that this book is going to explore. Religions provide guidelines on moral questions and answers to the hard questions. You should be willing to think through all the ideas and not reject or accept them before you have found out about them properly.

▼ *Learning how different religions answer these questions helps us to think through our own ideas and beliefs.*

▲ *'New Beginnings' by Shanti Panchal, 1998. We may understand this picture more if we recognise the Hindu god Ganesha in the background. (See page 33.)*

Where did I come from?

What's the meaning of life?

What's important in life?

Why do people have to suffer?

What happens after death?

2 In the USA it is illegal for state schools to teach about religion. What reasons do you think there might be for this policy?

3 Imagine that you live in a country where RE is not taught in schools and you wish to persuade people that the subject should be introduced. Design a leaflet to explain what RE is and why it is important.

Where can people look for God?

Is there a God? If so, what is God like? People have asked these questions for as long as human beings have been around. Most believers in God say that God is all-powerful, all-knowing, and all-good. In Unit 2 you will learn what some people say about how God reveals himself in people's lives. You will also consider other 'proofs' for the existence of God. You are to imagine that you are investigators. Your assignment is to investigate different evidence for the existence of God.

> Today the search goes on: 'The signs of online religious activity are everywhere. If you instruct AltaVista, a powerful internet search engine, to scour the Web for references to Microsoft's Bill Gates, the program turns up an impressive 25,000 references. But ask it to look for Web pages that mention God, and you'll get 410,000 hits.'
>
> *TIME* magazine, 16 December 1996

2.1

Looking for God – where do we start?

1 If you were to look for proof of God's existence where would you look? As a class, draw a spider diagram of your responses.

2 Make a glossary of key words related to belief and non-belief in the existence of God. Also make a class word bank – in the form of a display – so that the words are in front of you all the time.

Here are some key words about believers and non-believers:

A person who believes in God is a **theist**.

A person who does not believe in the existence of God is an **atheist**.

An **agnostic** believes that it is impossible to know if God exists – i.e. the person admits that he or she doesn't know whether God exists.

A **humanist** believes that it is possible to achieve happiness and fulfilment without religion.

A **pantheist** believes that God is in everything in nature and in the universe.

Before we start looking at evidence, we need to be clear about what we are looking for. In looking for God we are investigating religious matters. We therefore need to know what religious truth is and how this differs from other forms of truth. We could waste a lot of time if we started looking in the wrong places.

3 **a** The following is a list of things that people may believe are true. What type of truth is each? For each one, say whether it is a moral, religious, scientific, mathematical, historical, or personal truth.

I believe that:
- 2 + 2 = 4
- Smoking is harmful to health
- The purpose of life is to earn a lot of money
- Murder is wrong
- There is life after death
- Germany lost the Second World War

b Give one more example of each of the different types of truth.

c Rank the types of truths in order 1 to 6, with the most easy to believe at the top of the list and the most difficult at the bottom. Explain what you put at the top and bottom of your list, and why you put the truths in this order.

d Which of the six 'I believe that' statements is: (i) a fact, (ii) an opinion, and (iii) a belief? How can you tell?

e Do you think there is a difference between an opinion and a belief? If so, what is it?

4 Ask people at school and at home about different types of truth. You could start by asking your subject teachers to give you an example of truth in their subject – for instance, what is a scientific truth, an English truth, a geographical truth, etc?

5 As a result of the work you have done, try to complete the sentence: 'Religious truth is …'.
Share your statements as a class and arrive at a class definition.

Can God be experienced?

1 Think of examples of people having a religious experience. As a class, collect your ideas in a spider diagram.

Many religious people believe that God reveals himself to human beings. God does this in a variety of ways, including through sacred books [A], prayer [B], worship [C, D], visions and dreams [E], and conversion [F].

▲ Reading the Qur'an. Muslims believe that the words in the Qur'an came from Allah. They are Allah's message to humankind, telling them how to behave in the world.

source A

'Before reading the Qur'an, I prepare myself by washing certain parts of my body, and, if possible, wearing clean clothes. When I read the Qur'an I feel that Allah is really listening and is willing to guide me in what I should do. I read the Qur'an to find out what Allah wants me to do. Allah can see everything that I have gone through and loves me. Even when I feel very alone, as soon as I start reading the Qur'an I realise that I am not alone. I feel Allah close beside me, helping me to know what to do.'

Hamoudi, school student

Personal experiences shape the way we see the world. For example, if we are brought up in a happy home, it is likely that we will regard the world as a safe place. The opposite is likely to be true if we are brought up in a violent home. The same is the case with religious experiences. They help shape the way people see the world.

As you investigate the pictures and sources in this unit, consider what they tell you about each person's experience of God and how the experience influences their view of the world.

2 **a** In what ways do Muslims think that the Qur'an is a personal message to them from Allah?

b Why do you think some Muslims cry when they read the Qur'an?

c How might reading the Qur'an help someone who is feeling alone, or frightened?

d How do Muslims show respect for the Qur'an?

source B

'When I explain prayer to the children, I ask them how they get to know somebody. I think that the best way to get to know somebody is to talk to them, and listen to them. Prayer is a way of talking and listening to God – and so it is a really good way of getting to know him.'

Julia, junior school teacher

◄ Sikhs pray together during a service at the gurdwara. A prayer that is said at all Sikh services is called the 'ardas'. In this prayer, Sikhs remember God, the Sikh Gurus, and then all of humanity.

source C

'We believe that God is present in the images of gods and goddesses in temples and homes. When we worship, we come to have what we call darshan. This means to see God. The image is treated like an honoured royal guest.'

Kavita, age 17

3   'Prayer is a way of talking and listening to God.' How do you think God speaks to people through prayer? In what sense do people 'hear' God's voice?

4   What do you think it means to say that 'God is present in the images of gods and goddesses'? How do Hindus experience God in worship?

source D

'Each day we make offerings to God at the shrine. Before we worship, we get ready to meet God by washing and putting on clean clothes. We bathe and dress the image and put flowers around it. We say prayers and offer food.'

Dinesh, age 19

➤ Hindus worship at their home shrine.

Jacob's Ladder

Narrator: Jacob left Beersheba and set out for Haran. When he had reached a certain place, he stopped there for the night, since the sun had set. Taking one of the stones of that place, he made it his pillow and lay down where he was. He had a dream: there was a ladder, planted on the ground with its top reaching to heaven; and God's angels were going up and down on it. And there was Yahweh, standing beside him and saying,

Yahweh: I, Yahweh, am the God of Abraham your father, and the God of Isaac. The ground on which you are lying I shall give to you and your descendants. Your descendants will be as plentiful as the dust on the ground; you will spread out to west and east, to north and south, and all clans on earth will bless themselves by you and your descendants. Be sure, I am with you; I shall keep you safe wherever you go, and bring you back to this country, for I shall never desert you until I have done what I have promised you.

Narrator: Then Jacob woke from his sleep and said,

Jacob: (startled) Truly, Yahweh is in this place and I did not know.

Narrator: He was afraid and said,

Jacob: (afraid) How awe-inspiring this place is! This is nothing less than the abode of God, and this is the gate of heaven!

Narrator: Early next morning, Jacob took the stone he had used for his pillow, and set it up as a pillar, pouring oil over the top of it. He named the place Bethel, but before that the town had been called Luz. Jacob then made this vow,

Jacob: If God remains with me and keeps me safe on this journey I am making, if he gives me food to eat and clothes to wear, and if I come home safe to my father's home, then Yahweh shall be my God. This stone I have set up as a pillar is to be a house of God, and I shall faithfully pay you a tenth part of everything you give me.

dramatised version of
Genesis 28: 10-22, *The Jerusalem Bible*

4 a What type of religious experience is described in source E?

b In what sense is this experience true, to Jacob?

c What do you think Jewish people learn from this story? Why do you think it is important to the history of the Jewish people?

The conversion of Emperor Constantine

Constantine the Great was Roman emperor from 306 to 337 CE. His father had brought him up to worship the sun god Sol. Sol was thought to be the companion of the Roman emperor. However, in 312, the day before a battle with Maxentius, Constantine dreamed that Jesus Christ appeared to him and told him to write the first two letters of his name ('XP' in Greek) on the shields of his soldiers. The next day Constantine had a vision of a cross in the sky. It was positioned over the sun, together with the words 'In this sign you will be the victor.' Constantine went on to defeat Maxentius at the Battle of the Milvian Bridge, near Rome.

From this time, Constantine worshipped the Christian God. He put an end to the Roman persecution of Christians. In 313 he issued the Edict of Milan, which allowed Christians to practise their religion in the Roman Empire. Christianity became the official religion of the Roman Empire and the Church was given legal rights and large financial donations.

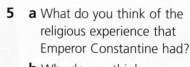

THIS TEA IS COLD!

LOOK! A FLYING SAUCER!

5   **a** What do you think of the religious experience that Emperor Constantine had?

b Why do you think Constantine started to believe in the Christian God as a result of his experience?

c How did this experience affect the Empire?

6   Many people report strange experiences of UFOs, demons, etc. How do we distinguish between true experiences and imaginary ones? Write out your thoughts in the form of 'Guidelines to help you distinguish between a true and false experience'.

What are the arguments for God's existence?

Look up at the stars in the night sky and you may feel like the man who wrote Psalm 19 [A]. But you may feel like Pascal, who was frightened [B].

source A

'The heavens declare the glory of God, the vault of heaven proclaims his handiwork.'

Psalm 19: 1

source B

The mathematician and physicist Blaise Pascal (1623-62) felt frightened by the immense size of the universe:

'The eternal silence of these infinite spaces terrifies me.'

1 a Does anything in nature fill you with awe and wonder?

   b Bring in to school a poem or a picture that you think expresses wonder at the universe. Say why it is important to you.

2 Read sources A and B. Which is closer to your own feelings? Why?

The universe is very big. It would take a ray of light about 15,000,000,000 years to travel across it, and light travels at 300,000,000 metres per second!

In all this vast universe, we know of only one tiny planet – Earth – where life exists. Conditions everywhere else in the universe make life, as we know it, impossible. The Sun is too hot, the Moon has no water, Jupiter is full of freezing gas, which is poisonous ... Some scientists tell us that, if the laws of physics were just a little bit different, there could be no life on Earth at all. And this can lead to the question: why are the laws of physics such that they make life possible?

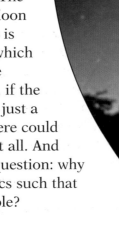

The argument from design

Some people say that it seems as if Planet Earth has been *designed* so that there can be human life. Some people say that the designer is God.

Many people say that there must be a designer behind the beauty, intricate detail, and order of nature. They might show you this bromeliad in the rainforest in Brazil as one example. Its colours, shape, and texture are beautiful. Rainwater collects in the 'bowl' formed by the bromeliad's leaves, and some bromeliads grow so big that insects and amphibians can live in the water. It is argued that the beautiful and clever design of the bromeliad, and all other things in nature, are evidence of a creator who designed the Earth to be the way it is. This creator is God.

That argument for the existence of God is called the 'argument from design'.

3 Not all people believe that the beauty and order of nature are evidence of one creator, an all-powerful, all-knowing, all-good God, who designed it all. In groups, share your thoughts on what problems the argument from design might have. What other explanations could there be for the beauty and order of the universe? Report your ideas to the class.

▲ *A bromeliad flowers in the canopy of the rainforest in Brazil.*

source C

'Consider each human being. Each person has their own DNA, which is like the language in the heart of the cell telling the cell how to construct proteins. The chemicals in DNA are grouped into "messenger molecules", which act like letters in a message. They must lie in a particular order if the message is going to be understood. Is this another example of how the universe is created by an intelligent designer?'

Sofia, age 26

What about natural disasters?

One of the main arguments against the argument from design is that the world is not always wonderful and beautiful, as many news articles show (D, E).

Volcano erupts in Guatemala

Pacaya shot lava 150 metres into the air, causing people to have to run from their homes in fear of their lives.

17 January 2000

▲ *Lava streams down the side of the Pacaya volcano.*

4 What explanations can you give for the events described in sources D and E?

5 Do you think that natural disasters like earthquakes and floods disprove the argument that the universe was created by God? Explain your answer.

6 The argument from design is one of the most frequently used arguments for the existence of God. Briefly write up two ideas in support of the argument from design and two ideas that weaken it.

Desperate search for quake victims

India's worst earthquake for fifty years has killed thousands of people. The earthquake measured between 6.9 and 7.9 on the Richter scale. It has caused widespread destruction in Gujarat and parts of neighbouring Pakistan.

28 January 2001

➤ *Houses destroyed by the earthquake in the village of Khavda.*

The cosmological argument

The cosmological argument is another well-known argument for the existence of God. 'Cosmos' means the universe. This argument states that absolutely everything has been caused by something before it. The universe is a result of a series of causes and effects. At the very beginning of these there must have been the very first cause – and this was God.

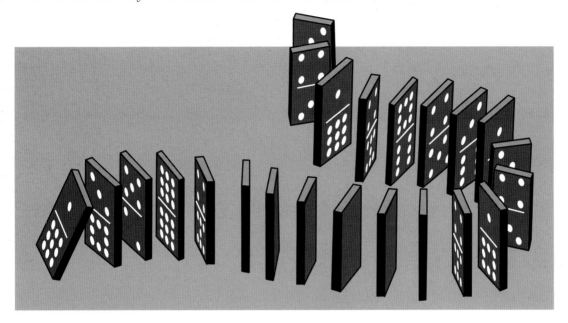

7 What will happen when the first domino falls against the next one? In groups, list other examples illustrating cause and effect.

8 Why do you think that some people would say that the cosmological argument does not prove God's existence?

9 Does this argument for the existence of God give any idea of what God is like?

What is faith?

People believe in God, even if the existence of God cannot be proved. This is called having faith [F, G].

source F

'All arguments for the existence or non-existence of God leave the matter open, and belief in God is a matter of interpreting experience one way rather than another.'

Bishop Richard Harries,
Questioning Belief, 1995

source G

'Belief in God is a matter of faith. Some people trust in money and material things to bring happiness and live their lives according to this philosophy, even though the evidence suggests that those material things don't necessarily bring happiness. I have faith in God, and live my life according to this faith.'

Mark, school student

You have now looked at three arguments for the existence of God: (1) the argument from religious experience (Unit 2.2), (2) the argument from design, and (3) the cosmological argument. Use the following activities to sum up what you have found.

10 a In groups, make a short list of everyday things that you have faith in and do not question – for example, faith that, when you cross the road, cars will stop. Explain how this faith affects how you live on a daily basis.

b In what sense is believing in God a matter of faith?

-5 -4 -3 -2 -1 0 1 2 3 4 5

I don't
believe
in God

I'm
not
sure

I
believe in
God

11 Copy the 'Belief Line' above.

a Show where (i) a theist, (ii) an atheist, and (iii) an agnostic would mark themselves on this Belief Line.

b Mark yourself on the Belief Line.

c Give reasons for your position.

d What evidence in this unit (i) supports your opinion and (ii) is the opposite of your opinion?

12 Imagine what it would take for you to change your opinion. Use the writing frame on the right to prepare a speech for a debate.

I think that ... because ...

The reasons why I have made this decision are, first ... so

Another reason is ...

In order for me to change my mind I would need to know ... and experience ...

Unit 3

Religious language

When talking about religious ideas and experiences, people often find that words aren't enough to express all that they mean. There need to be other ways of explaining. In Unit 3 we will think about the ways of communicating that we use every day, in addition to speaking. Then we will look at signs and symbols that are used to express religious truths.

3.1

Speaking without words

Signs and symbols

A sign gives information about something in a simple way that is easy to recognise. Think of a no-smoking sign, road signs, shop and restaurant signs, and many more. Also think of how a gesture or a look on someone's face can be a sign of their mood. Sometimes people use their clothes as a sign to say something about themselves.

A symbol is a particular kind of sign. It is a picture or an object which represents something more than itself. We recognise the Union Jack flag as a symbol for the United Kingdom and the £ symbol, which stands for 'pounds'. Political parties, charities, and other organisations often devise symbols to represent their outlook and activities.

The swastika is an example of a symbol whose meaning has changed through history and as it has been used in different cultures across the world. The symbol consists of a cross with its four arms bent at right angles. In Hinduism, it is often explained as a symbol of the changing world around the fixed, unchanging centre of God. It is also thought to be a symbol of the sun and is used as a sign of good fortune

▲ *For Hindus, the swastika is used as a symbol of good fortune.*

▽ *In the 1930s, the Nazi party adopted the swastika as their symbol. This cartoon of the Nazi leader Adolf Hitler was saying that the Nazis had spoilt the symbol.*

during ceremonies such as weddings. Unfortunately, in the twentieth century, the symbol was adopted by the Nazi party in Germany and then became associated with cruelty, racism, and narrow-mindedness – the opposites of Hindu values.

What are we saying with our bodies?

We don't 'speak' only with our voices but also with our body gestures. At a rough estimate we make at least 3,000 different gestures using our hands and fingers. Body language is symbolic. It represents visually what the person is thinking and feeling as well as saying. Sometimes a person says one thing, but expresses something quite different with their body language. The many small gestures we make reveal our mood and what we are really feeling.

> **1** What can you tell about this character's mood from his gestures? Try writing a caption for each picture.

> **2** What do the following gestures tell you about a person's mood?
> - shaking hands
> - clenched fist
> - pointing finger
> - thumbing the nose
> - prodding forefinger
>
> You could make this exercise into a game in which your fellow students have to guess what you are trying to say.
>
> **3** Two people in a room without a common spoken language will soon communicate with one another by means of body language. Try this out yourselves. In twos, try communicating for three minutes using no words. Then individually write up an account of what you think you communicated. Share your accounts. How close were they to each other? What does this teach you about body language?

In a television programme called *The Human Animal*, in 1994, the anthropologist Desmond Morris presented a study of human behaviour. From interviewing many different groups of people he concluded that most parts of the body have symbolic meaning for different cultures. These are his findings:

- Eyes: sometimes stand for the sun or the all-seeing eye of God. The eye is the window of the soul and the light of the body.

- Head: often regarded as the seat of the life force. People in charge are known as the head of the organisation. In Asia, people bow their heads when they greet each other, as a sign of respect.

- Ears: in the East royalty wore large, heavy earrings which pulled their earlobes down. The Buddha is usually shown with long ears as a sign that he was a prince. Long earlobes are symbols of authority and royalty.

- Hair: often symbolises strength and energy. Many Buddhist monks and nuns shave their head as a sign of humility. They are following the action of the Buddha who shaved off his hair as a sign that he did not rely on worldly strength.

▼ *Whereas Buddhist monks shave their heads, Sikhs (left) follow the example of the Sikh Gurus and never cut their hair.*

- Heart: in Christianity the heart symbolises love, joy, and compassion. In ancient Greece the heart was the centre of thought, feeling, and will. In Islam it is the spiritual centre.

- Hands: hand gestures can symbolise many things, for example protection, friendship, authority. People speak of giving a 'helping hand'. Holding hands is a sign of love.

The same gesture is understood in different ways in different parts of the world. For example, touching the earlobe ...

> ... in Portugal, means that something is excellent, magnificent

> ... in Italy, means the man referred to is effeminate

> ... in Spain, means that someone is a 'sponger' and never pays for his drinks

> ... in other countries, can mean 'I will box your ears'.

He needs LOVE

Cupid's arrow pierces the heart, the seat of love. The victim experiences the unexpected pleasure and pain of desire.

4 What do people mean when they use the V sign today? What was its original meaning?

5 Become a 'people watcher' and over the next 24 hours make an ethogram of human actions. An ethogram is a list of characteristic movements, gestures, facial expressions, and body postures. Watch people in their everyday environments. What does your ethogram say about people? You could take photos (with people's permission!) to share with the class.

The V sign

According to historians, this gesture can be traced to an incident in 1415, before the battle of Agincourt. The French threatened that when they won the battle they would cut off the 'bow fingers' of all the defeated English archers. This meant the first and second fingers, which were used to draw the bow, and so the archers would be prevented from ever firing a bow again. The English king, Henry V, warned his archers and their anger at the French threat made them go into battle with greater determination. The English won, and the English archers mocked the French by holding up their still-attached bow fingers.

3.2

Speaking of God

Just as symbols are important tools for communicating in everyday life, so also they are used by religions to communicate about God and spiritual realities. Religious symbols communicate ideas at a deep intuitive level. They work with people's feelings as well as their thoughts.

How is light used as a symbol of God?

1 Brainstorm the word 'light'. List all the things you can think of, associated with light. Use a dictionary search of 'light' to add further words.

2 Light is a powerful symbol because it has many qualities. What do 'seeing the light at the end of the tunnel' and 'becoming enlightened' mean?

Light is a common symbol for God:

> source A
>
> The Muslim holy book, the Qur'an, compares Allah to light: 'Allah is the light of the heavens and the earth ... Allah guides to His light whom He will ...'
>
> *Qur'an 24*

> source B
>
> The Hindu holy book, the Gita, says of God: 'Could a thousand suns blaze forth together it would be a faint reflection of the radiance of God.'
>
> *Bhagavad Gita 11: 12*

> source C
>
> The Christian holy book, the Bible, says: 'God is light, and in him there is no darkness at all.'
>
> *1 John 1: 5*

3 Light helps people to see. Darkness makes it difficult or impossible to see. You could say that darkness makes you blind. What do you think it means to say that someone is:
   - physically blind
   - morally blind
   - spiritually blind?
Provide examples to illustrate your answers.

In religious language, when God is described as light, this means more than physical light. God is the source of spiritual light, of truth.

In Christianity, Jesus, as the Son of God, is also described as bringing light. The Christian Bible tells that Jesus healed a blind man (John, chapter 9). Christians understand that the man gained not only physical sight but also spiritual insight – he came to believe that Jesus was the Messiah sent from God and he started to worship him.

Holman Hunt's painting 'The Light of the World' is based on some words of Jesus: 'I am the light of the world. Whoever follows me will have the light of life and will never walk in darkness.' (John 8: 12). Hunt uses a variety of symbols. The lantern stands for Jesus as the source of light. It is night, showing that Jesus brings light into the dark world of the sinner. Hunt explained that 'the closed door was the obstinately shut mind; the weeds the cumber of daily neglect ... the bat flitting about only in darkness was a natural symbol of ignorance'. Asked why the door had no outside handle, he replied: 'It is the door of the human heart, and that can only be opened from the inside.'

▲ 'The Light of the World', painted by Holman Hunt in 1900.

4 Read Revelation 3: 20. Write a short paragraph explaining how Holman Hunt's painting is also based on this verse.

5 Light is such an important religious symbol that it is central to several festivals. Research *one* of the following festivals to find out (a) how and (b) why light is used in the festival: Hanukkah – a Jewish festival; Christmas – a Christian festival; Diwali – a Hindu festival.

Why do some religions use images to represent God?

Sometimes religions use images to represent God. For example, in a church you may see a picture of a dove, representing the Holy Spirit. For Christians, the Holy Spirit is God's living presence with people today. Christians talk about God as Father, Son, and Holy Spirit.

A dove is a symbol of peace. The Holy Spirit is shown as a dove because it brings peace between people and God.

The elephant-headed god Ganesha symbolises the power to overcome obstacles. Hindus turn to Ganesha when seeking help to overcome feelings such as jealousy and anger.

Hindu homes and temples have many sacred images, like this one of Ganesha. How do these help people to talk about God? Hindus believe that spirit, called Brahman, is present in and supports the entire universe, but cannot be seen. Brahman is conscious, eternal, and unchanging. Many Hindus translate 'Brahman' as God. They believe that Brahman is present in the sacred images, and so the images make it possible for them to see and interact with God.

6 In the same way as a photo can bring to life memories and feelings about a loved one, so the sacred image of a Hindu god can make God's presence seem real. What qualities of Ganesha do you think are represented by the objects he is holding?

Is life a struggle between good and evil?

◄ *On 11 September 2001 a terrorist attack on the World Trade Centre in New York killed more than 3,000 people. The attack, and those who carried it out, were described as evil.*

source A

In response to the terrorist attacks on the USA on 11 September 2001, Britain's Christian, Muslim, and Jewish leaders made a joint statement:

'We and all people of good faith and goodwill – whatever their religious, ethnic, or racial background – are appalled by these terrible attacks. Such evil deeds have no place in the world we seek to share. As Christian, Jewish, and Muslim religious leaders, we believe that it is vital amid so much anguish and suffering to nourish all that we hold common and to resist all that would drive us apart.'

How would you explain what evil is? You might think of examples like the cruel behaviour of parents who abuse their children; or the way the Serbs in Bosnia used 'ethnic cleansing' to try to get rid of non-Serbs in their country. One view that runs through several religions is that what happens in the world is part of a continuing battle between good and evil.

Have you seen *Superman* or *Star Wars*? Both these films illustrate a battle between good and evil. Good and evil are qualities that are difficult to represent as pictures. This may be one reason why the films use extraordinary, 'unreal' imagery: in one case the superhero has supernatural powers; in the other the battle is set in outer space. In real life, the idea is that the battle between good and evil goes on within us.

1 **a** Why do you think films like *Star Wars* and *Superman* are popular?

b Can you think of other films or books about good versus evil?

2 Choose a recent newspaper. Cut out all the stories that are about (a) 'good' news events, (b) 'bad' news events. Use headlines and photos to make a collage of the battle between good and evil.

3 Some people argue that people are affected by watching violent images on television and video. Do you agree? Do you think there is a relationship between what you watch and what you become?

The Ramayana – a triumph for good

Some religions tell symbolic stories illustrating the battle between good and evil. One of the best-known collections of Hindu stories is the *Ramayana* – the story of Rama. It was written in Sanskrit, probably no later than the third century BCE and possibly much earlier. The *Ramayana* relates the adventures of Rama. Many Hindus believe the stories, which are considered to come from God.

source B

Rama and Sita

Long ago in India there lived a king called Dasharatha. He was loved by all. Dasharatha had three queens. The first gave birth to a son, Rama. The second gave birth to a son, Bharat. The third had twin boys, Lakshmana and Shatrughan. Rama married Sita, the most beautiful princess of a neighbouring kingdom, after winning a competition to bend and string the great heavy bow of Siva. For twelve years Rama and Sita lived happily. Everyone loved Rama.

As Dasharatha grew older, he decided to retire and make Rama the king of Koshal. But things did not go to plan. Dasharatha's second wife became jealous and started planning to have her own son, Bharat, crowned king instead. A long time before, she had saved Dasharatha's life during a war and afterwards he had granted her two wishes. She now used both wishes, asking for Bharat to be crowned king and for Rama to be sent into exile in the forest for fourteen years.

As a pious and noble king, Dasharatha had always kept his word. He sent for Rama and told him the news. Rama replied, 'I am happy to follow your order and to honour your promise. Let Bharat rule. I will leave for the forest immediately.' Dasharatha died, his heart broken. When Bharat heard that it was his own mother who was the cause of the disaster, he turned away from her in disgust.

Meanwhile, Surpanakha fell in love with Rama, and asked him to be her husband. She was the sister of a powerful demon king, called Ravana, who lived on the island of Sri Lanka. Rama was amused, saying that he was already married, but Surpanakha was furious at being rejected. Coming to his sister's aid, Ravana decided to abduct Sita. He disguised himself as a hermit. Sita came out with a bowl of rice to offer to the holy man. Ravana pounced on Sita and whisked her away on his chariot to Sri Lanka.

Rama went in search of the monkey king Sugrive, to help him get Sita back. Sugrive ordered his monkey army to search for Sita. Hanuman, the monkey general, found Sita, crying, in one of Ravana's gardens. Hanuman confronted Ravana: 'You have abducted the wife of my all-powerful master, Lord Rama. If you want peace, return her to my master with honour or else you and your kingdom will be destroyed.' Ravana refused. Rama, with the monkey army, built a bridge across the water to Sri Lanka and invaded Ravana's kingdom. In a fierce battle Rama killed Ravana. He rescued Sita and, after the fourteen years of exile were over, Bharat came to escort Rama and Sita back home. When they reached home, the entire city celebrated. Thousands of lamps were lit and Rama was made king.

For many Hindus, Rama is the ideal king, husband, and warrior. He is one of the most popular gods in Hinduism. His victory over Ravana is regarded as a triumph of good over evil. The story is celebrated each

The lights at Diwali stand for the lanterns that were lit on Rama's return to his kingdom.

year at the Hindu festival of Diwali, the festival of light. This takes place in the darkest part of the year, in October or November, and lasts up to five days. Lamps and fireworks are used. For many Hindus, Diwali is the most important festival of the year and coincides with their New Year.

The story of Rama is rich in meaning for Hindus. Rama is a perfect example of an obedient son. He willingly undertook hardship to save his father's honour. He was also a great warrior, standing for what was right. Ravana's defeat illustrates the fate of those who consider God's property their own. Sita was Rama's property and Ravana stole her. Hanuman, the monkey general, stands for strength, courage, and loyalty.

Today, Rama is often worshipped as an *avatar*, or incarnation, of Vishnu.

4 Find out more about the festival of Diwali. Imagine that you are a reporter for a newspaper, sent to cover the celebration of the festival. Write a short article for your paper in which you include:

- an account of what Diwali celebrates
- how the festival is celebrated
- an explanation of any special symbolic objects used to celebrate the festival
- an explanation of why Diwali is considered a celebration of good over evil
- quotes from people you have interviewed, saying what the festival means to them.

5 Find out about Brahma, Vishnu, and Shiva, and their *avatars* or appearances on earth.

6 Write your own mythical story for children, illustrating the triumph of good over evil. Design it in the form of a booklet with pictures. Keep your sentences short and try to make the booklet enjoyable for young children.

7 Do you think the image of a battle between good and evil is an effective one to describe events in the world?

How did the universe begin?

In Unit 4 you will meet different ideas about the way the universe began – religious creation stories and scientific accounts. You will investigate whether or not the religious and scientific accounts are in conflict and whether it is possible to hold religious beliefs in a scientific age.

4.1

What do creation stories tell us?

1 Hold a class discussion about how you think the universe came into being.

People have always tried to explain how the universe began. Different cultures have told different creation stories, conveying major parts of their beliefs [A]. Over a hundred and fifty years ago scientists provided additional accounts of the beginning of the world – the theories of the Big Bang and evolution.

Today different branches of science can explain many things, such as why the weather behaves as it does and why people behave as they do. But there are still some larger questions that are difficult – or even impossible – for science to answer. Why is there a world? Why did the human race come into being? Why do people have longings for something bigger and greater 'out there'? Religious creation stories may hold some answers.

The Iroquois creation story

The Iroquois are a group of six Native American nations. Native Americans often speak of the earth and animals as their family. All things in creation are closely related to each other. The earth is sometimes referred to as a mother, since she is a source of life. This means that the earth must be protected and not exploited.

source A

Skywoman

Before this earth existed, there was a place in the sky where beings lived who did not know what it was to cry, feel pain, or die. They lived in lodges with their families.

In this land in the sky there lived an ancient chief, whose wife was expecting a child. The chief became sick, although no one in the Sky World knew what it was to be sick. As time passed, he became weaker and died. He was put in a burial case, which was placed near the ceiling of his house.

His wife gave birth to a female being who was named Aientsik, which means Fertile Earth. Although the child was healthy, one day she began to cry. The people of the village could do nothing to make her stop. So her mother placed her in front of the burial case. She stopped crying. This happened many times.

One day Aientsik came back from visiting her father and told her mother that she was to be married. The next day the young woman set out with gifts for the village where Tharonhiawakon, or He Who Holds Up the Sky, lived. She offered him the gifts and he agreed to marry her.

She stayed with him three nights, but then her husband began to feel sick. He had a dream which made him feel uncomfortable. He gathered the people of his village together and told them the meaning of the dream.

The next morning the man took Aientsik to a tall beautiful tree. It was always laden with fruit and blossoms. He told all the young men in the village to uproot the tree. A large hole was created. As Aientsik leaned forward to see what was below, the man pushed her into the hole. Alarmed, she grabbed for help and took the roots of the strawberry tree with her as she fell.

She fell into darkness for some time, but soon she could see water below her, with animals in it. Two swans flew up to rescue her, catching her between their wings. Other birds realised that she did not have webbed feet like them and could therefore not survive in the water. They asked the Turtle if she could land on his back. The Turtle agreed.

A muskrat dived below the waters. He had heard that there was earth far below. He brought back some earth and placed it on the Turtle's back so that Aientsik would have somewhere to stand. Every day Aientsik walked around the edge of the Turtle's back. Each day the earth on which she was standing grew bigger until it became the whole world. Soon plants started to grow from the roots she had grabbed when she had fallen into this world. Life on earth had begun.

Aientsik gave birth to a daughter, and two children were then born to Aientsik's daughter. One was called Good Mind and the other Evil Mind. Good Mind gave the earth the elm trees, springs of pure water, flowers, and butterflies. Evil Mind gave muddy water, briars, poisonous insects, and snakes. When her daughter died, Aientsik became so sad that she left the earth and became Grandmother Moon.

2 Why do you think this creation story is called 'Skywoman'? What is the meaning of 'Aientsik'? Why is this name important? According to this story, why was the world created? What is the role of animals in this creation? What is the role of Aientsik, the Skywoman? What does she bring? What is the nature of her two grandchildren? What do you think this story is trying to explain?

Just a week's work – or was it? The Jewish and Christian creation story

Jews and Christians believe that God is the creator and cares for everything in the universe. An account of how the world was created, in six days, is found at the beginning of the Bible, in the first chapter of Genesis. Source B is part of a modern version of this story. It is from 'The Creation' by the American poet James Weldon Johnson.

▼ *An illustration of the creation of light from an eighteenth-century Bible.*

source B

And God stepped out on space,
And he looked around and said,
"I'm lonely –
I'll make me a world."

And as far as the eye of God could see
Darkness covered everything,
Blacker than a hundred midnights
Down in a cypress swamp.

Then God smiled,
And the light broke,
And the darkness rolled up on one side,
And the light stood shining on the other,
And God said, "That's good!"

... Then God walked around
And God looked around
On all that He had made.
He looked at His sun,
And he looked at His moon,
And he looked at His little stars;
He looked on His world
With all its living things,
And God said, "I'm lonely still."

... God thought and thought,
Till He thought, "I'll make me a man!"

Up from the bed of the river
God scooped the clay;
And by the bank of the river
He kneeled Him down;
And there the God Almighty
Who lit the sun and fixed it in the sky,
Who flung the stars to the most far corner of the night,
Who rounded the earth in the middle of His hand –
This Great God,
Like a mammy bending over her baby,
Kneeled down in the dust
Toiling over a lump of clay
Till he shaped it in His own image;

Then into it He blew the breath of life,
And man became a living soul.
Amen. Amen.

3 Make a list of the verbs used in the poem to describe God's actions. What do they tell you about the act of creation?

4 According to the poem, why did God create the world? What do you think about this reason?

God's world

According to the Jewish and Christian creation story, God placed man and woman on the earth and gave them the first job description: 'God took the man and settled him in the garden of Eden to cultivate and take care of it.' (Genesis 2: 15)

The creation of the universe was completed in six days. On the seventh day God rested. God blessed the seventh day and set it apart as a special day.

This creation story speaks of a God who loves what was created. God stands apart from his creation, but the created world is covered with God's 'fingerprints'.

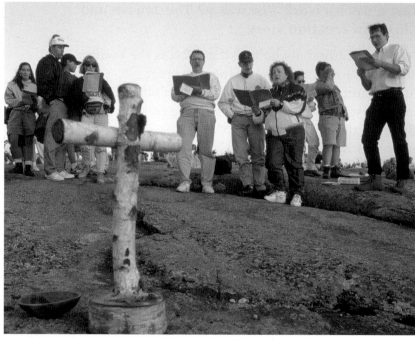

▲ *For Christians, Sunday is the day of the week that is 'set apart' for God. These people have gathered for an open-air service of worship.*

▼ *In what ways do humans have power over animals?*

5 Read the creation account in Genesis, chapter 1. What do you think is meant by 'And God saw that it was good'? Name four beautiful things in nature. Choose a flower and make a detailed drawing of it.

6 What do the creation accounts in Genesis say about (a) people's relationship to animals, (b) the relationship between God and humans?

7 Genesis 1: 26 says that God created humans in his image – that is, like himself. What do you think this means? In what ways might people be considered to be like God? Do you think that humans are more important than other animals?

8 Jews and Christians believe that one day a week should be set aside for God. Find out why Jews observe this day of rest on Saturday and Christians on Sunday. Find out some of the ways in which Jews and Christians mark the day.

9 Do you think the biblical account of creation is history or poetry or myth or some other form of literature? Do you think any of the language in the account is symbolic? If so, which symbols are used?

Different understandings

Different people understand the creation accounts in Genesis in different ways.

source C

'Creation happened exactly as it says in the Bible, in six days.'

Helen, school student

Day 1: Light
   Day 2: The sky
      Day 3: Land and seas and plants
         Day 4: Sun, moon, and stars
            Day 5: Fish and birds
               Day 6: Animals and humans

source D

'The creation account is not to be read in a literal way. For example, the word "day" means something longer than 24 hours. The sequence of creation agrees with scientific accounts. The six days refer to the way in which the universe developed in an orderly way over time.'

Peter, school student

source E

'This creation story was written to tell you *why* the world was created, not *how* the world was created. It tells you that people are God's creations and are therefore to be treated well. Men and women were both created by God and are equal. It tells you that God was happy with creation. It tells you how people should treat animals and the world in which they live. The story tells you that the universe is not an accident – it was created by God for a purpose.'

Jane, school student

source F

Church leaders question creation stories

In a survey by BBC Radio 4's 'Today' programme, church leaders were asked whether they believed in the creation stories in the Bible. Out of 103 church leaders who took part in the survey, only three said that they believed, literally, in the biblical account that God created the world in six days.

December 1999

source G

'In Jewish thinking today there are a variety of ways of understanding the creation stories. Onc view is that the whole creation was performed on the first day and emerged on the earth's surface within the subsequent seven days. Others accept that the six days of creation are symbolic for six periods of time. They say that the creation story teaches us the main idea that God created this planet and all its life out of nothing and was not bound by considerations of time and place. What is important for Judaism is the acceptance that God created the world and made human beings responsible for treating the world well.'

Jacob, teacher

10 Do you think that the universe was created in six days? Explain your views.

11 Invent a new annual festival called 'Creation Day'. Describe how you would celebrate it. What would it celebrate?

Sikh beliefs about creation

Sikhism teaches that God existed before the world was created. God deliberately created all things; the universe came from God. God is present in creation and in human beings, but God is also more than the created world. Sikhs believe that God is Love and that he created the universe as an act of love [H, I, J, K].

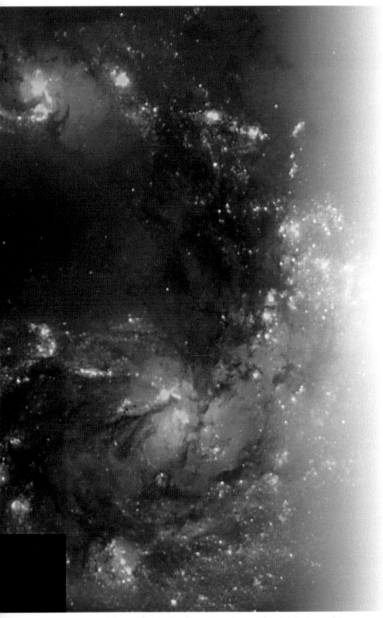

▲ *This image was taken by the Hubble space telescope. It shows two spiral galaxies colliding, about 63,000,000 light years away from Earth. The collision creates more than 1,000 star clusters.*

Sikhs see no disagreement between their beliefs and science, which shows that the universe has evolved over a long time and continues to develop. Guru Nanak, the founder of Sikhism, taught about 'an ever-becoming universe' [L, M].

source M

'From the external being the air evolved, and from gas comes the water. From the water were created three worlds and in every heart He infused His Light.'

Guru Granth Sahib 19

12 a How do Sikhs describe God's relationship to the creation? Is this a different understanding from the Jewish and Christian view? Explain your answer.

b How do Sikhs explain the relationship between their creation account and evolution? How would they answer the key question of this unit: is it possible to hold religious beliefs in a scientific age?

13 How might their belief in a creator God affect Sikhs' attitude to the environment today?

Make your own creation story

Work with a partner to make up your own creation story. In doing so you should learn more about yourself, because you will be talking about things that you hold dear. Your story should try to answer the basic questions of who, what, where, when, why, and how.

You may find it helpful to follow these stages:

- Read through some different creation stories. Some useful websites are listed here. You could print out the stories you find and underline the passages that you feel are the most important. Or you could copy and paste the important passages to a file on your computer. Remember to write down or copy and paste the URL of the file you take each passage from, so that you can quickly refer back to it if you need to.

- Use the information you have collected, facts, opinions, etc., to create an interesting creation story of your own. Use a word processor to write it up.

Some useful websites

http://www.indians.org/welker/creation.htm
http://www.dreamscape.com/morgana/ariel.htm
http://www.dreamscape.com/morgana/cordelia.htm
http://www.dreamscape.com/morgana/miranda.htm
http://www.dreamscape.com/morgana/umbriel.htm
http://www.bluecloud.org/32.html

How do scientists explain the universe?

The Big Bang

Many scientists believe that the universe started about 15 billion years ago with a Big Bang. A gigantic explosion caused matter to expand outwards, and the universe, as we know it, was formed. At this time the atmospheric conditions were harsh. For example, there was no oxygen. The environment was unsuitable for life as we know it.

▲ Scientists Arno Penzias and Robert Wilson stand by the horn antenna that they used to detect cosmic radiation; New Jersey, USA.

source A

Big Bang: proof

For years scientists tried to find evidence to support the theory that the universe began with an explosion of matter, called the 'Big Bang'. In 1992 they achieved what they wanted: they were able to measure slight ripples of cosmic radiation. The scientists explained that these ripples are evidence of the cooling-off process that has been going on for millions of years since the explosion first produced a hot ball of gas, giving off radiation.

1 Do you think the Big Bang theory is a good explanation of how the universe began?

2 What caused the Big Bang explosion? Was there anything before the Big Bang?

source B

'The Cosmos is all that is or ever was or ever will be.'

from Carl Sagan, *Cosmos* (1980)

The first signs of life

Many scientists believe that the first signs of life appeared on earth 2,800,000,000 years ago. They think that living organisms developed from molecules found in a watery mixture that covered the surface of the earth. Scientists call this mixture the 'primordial soup'. Eventually the living organisms began to develop into more and more complex forms, and finally into human beings. Humans are the high point of this development, with the intelligence to control nature.

Different species

Charles Darwin was a British naturalist who took part in a scientific expedition on a ship called HMS *Beagle*. During the voyage, from 1831 to 1836, Darwin observed how animals and plants were suited to their environment. His most famous observations were made in the Galapagos Islands, off the west coast of South America. He thought that species must have changed over time in order to adapt to conditions on particular islands. For example, he thought that the ground finch had developed in different ways in different places, in order to survive in new environments. In this way, new species of finch had developed.

Most people in Darwin's time believed that all species had been made exactly as they were, by God. But Darwin concluded that species were not fixed: they changed in order to survive in changing environments, and, over millions of years, new species were produced. Darwin called this changing through time 'evolution'.

Darwin observed that the finches on each island of the Galapagos were suited to the particular feeding opportunities of that island. He made drawings to record his observations. The finches' beaks were differently shaped, depending on whether they fed on insects, or seeds, or plants. Darwin suspected that all the different types of finches had evolved from the large ground finch.

Evolution explained

Darwin came up with an idea to explain how species evolved. In 1859 he set out this idea in a book called *The Origin of Species by Means of Natural Selection.* He explained that some organisms are better suited to their environment than others. He then suggested that the better-suited organisms are more likely to survive long enough to breed. This is sometimes called the 'survival of the fittest'. The process by which the fittest survive occurs because of nature, so he called it 'natural selection'. We now understand this theory in terms of genes. Darwin later suggested that man evolved from apes. This came as a shock to many churchgoers. Some people stopped believing in God. If man had evolved from a monkey could he have been specially created by God?

Darwin's studies led him to believe that humans had evolved from lower members of the animal kingdom.

An example

The peppered moth is a good example of an organism adapting to survive in its environment. Originally the moth was light in colour, in order to merge with the bark of trees. Over time some dark-coloured moths appeared. Their darkness made them easier to see and the birds would catch and eat them.

However, in the Industrial Revolution, which took place in England in the nineteenth century, smoke from factories caused tree bark to become dark, and so it now gave camouflage to the darker moths. The lighter moths became the ones that were eaten by birds and the black moths increased in numbers and became the dominant form.

Understanding evolution

Different people understand evolution in different ways [C, D, E].

▲ *Light and dark peppered moths on the bark of a tree.*

source C

'God created the process of evolution. Evolution was the way in which God brought different species into the world.'

Simon, a priest

source D

'The forces of nature alone explain why everything exists. Evolution is nothing to do with God. Nature drew together the chemicals that formed the first living cell. Nature used a process of evolution to develop complex life-forms.'

Raja, university student

source E

'The likelihood of life beginning by chance is about as great as a hurricane blowing through a scrap yard and assembling a Rolls-Royce.'

The Prince of Wales, quoted in *The Sunday Times*, 26 December 2000

3 Draw a cartoon strip telling the scientific story of the beginning of the universe and how animal life developed.

4 What does it mean to say that organisms adapt to their environment? What does it mean to say that organisms are evolving?

5 Choose one animal and one plant and describe how each is adapted to its environment.

6 Compare the scientific explanation of the beginning of life with Sikh beliefs (pages 44-45). In what ways are they similar?

7 If men and women are descended from apes, are they only 'animals'?

8 **a** Must the idea of natural selection mean that God the Creator does not exist?

b Is it possible to hold religious beliefs in a scientific age?

Are there different ways of seeing the truth?

1 What do you see in each of these pictures? Is there more than one way of seeing each picture? If there is, which way of seeing is correct?

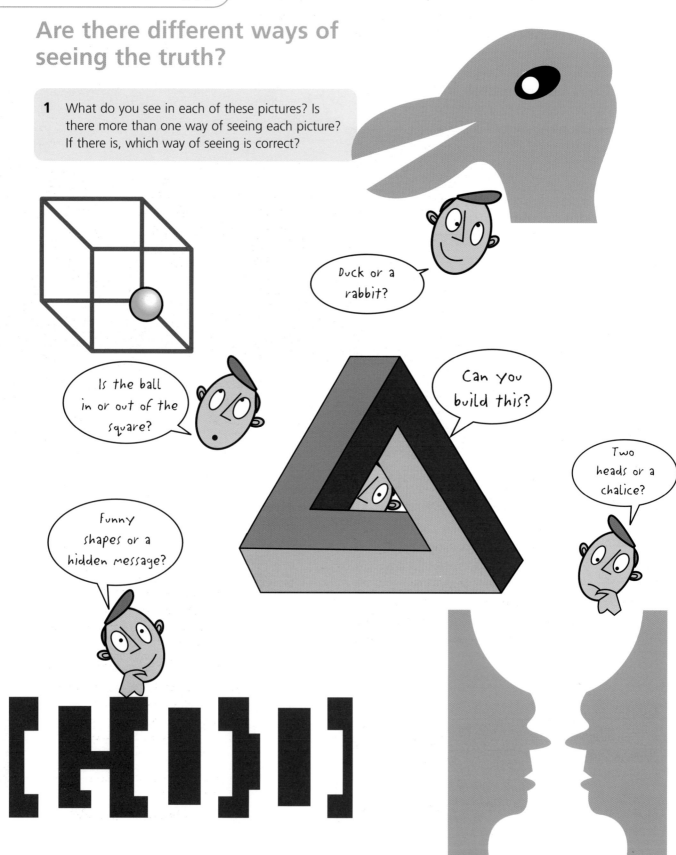

The pictures on the left are optical illusions. They show that the same picture can be seen in different ways. The same is true of much of life. An event can be seen, or 'understood', in different ways – and it isn't possible to say that any one way of seeing is right or wrong.

How might supporters from different sides 'see' this game in different ways?

In this unit we have looked at religious and scientific accounts of how the universe began. The accounts differ because they are intended to do different things. Some people say that science attempts to answer *how* the universe was made and religion attempts to answer *why* the universe was made [A].

source A

'There are questions scientists cannot answer – and never will be able to – questions like "has the universe a purpose?" We need to find that out from somewhere else.'

from M. Poole, *Science and Belief* (1990)

2 a Choose one of the religious creation accounts from Unit 4.1 and compare it with the scientific account (Unit 4.2). What do the two accounts have in common?

b How do the two accounts differ?

c Write down the most important point of each of the two accounts. Explain why you think these points are the most important.

d What kinds of truth do the two accounts contain?

e What is believable and why?

Understanding different types of writing

There are many types of writing. History, poetry, romantic fiction, scientific articles, and news reports are some examples. Each type of writing has its own style. When we read something, we can only understand properly what the writer is saying if we know what type of writing it is.

3 **a** Make a list of all the types of writing you can think of.

   b Choose three types and write two sentences of each type of writing.

   c Show your three pieces of writing to a partner and ask them to work out which types of writing they are. Get them to explain how they can tell.

4 Try to write about an emotion, such as anger or love, as if you were (a) the person who is experiencing the emotion, (b) a songwriter, (c) a scientist studying human behaviour.
How do your three pieces of writing differ? What kind of truth does each piece contain?

IT'S DAWN- GO FOR IT DADDYO HOT!

▲ *Is this what the writer of Job meant by 'the joyful concert of the morning stars'?*

Misunderstandings can occur if you don't know what type of writing you are reading. For example, in the Bible, the first verse of Psalm 93 says: 'The world is indeed set firm; it can never be shaken'. What type of writing is this? Did the writer mean that he thought the world was stuck together with glue, or made of jelly? What about this: 'the joyful concert of the morning stars' (Job 38: 7)? Does the picture on this page show what this really means? Religious texts are full of passages like this. Religious texts are not scientific journals, but use poetry, imagery, and story [B].

source B

'The Biblical creation narratives must not be used as a scientific account. They are concerned with theological [religious] truths.'

Sam Berry, Professor of Genetics, in M. Poole, *Science and Belief* (1990)

5 How do scientific and religious accounts of the origins of the universe differ? What questions is science trying to answer? What questions are religious accounts trying to answer?

6 Where do you think the universe came from? Use the information in Unit 4 to help you write a one-paragraph statement giving your reasons.

4.4

Are science and religion in conflict?

For the last thousand years or so, with regard to ideas about the universe, science and religion have been like brothers and sisters – sometimes arguing [A], at other times agreeing. Are religion and science conflicting opposites, or do they complement each other?

1 Which of these questions needs a scientific answer? Which needs a religious answer?
   - How do you make a chemical bomb?
   - Should chemical bombs be used in war?
   - How did the universe begin?
   - Did God create the universe?

2 Is it always necessary to make a choice between the scientific and religious answers to questions?

source A

New science ideas shake old beliefs

In 1633, the Christian Church punished the astronomer Galileo for teaching that the Earth moves around the Sun. This new idea, introduced by another astronomer, Copernicus, in 1543, was shocking to the Christian Church. Until then, people believed that the Earth was at the centre of God's universe.

Galileo was put under house arrest to prevent him teaching the new idea.

In 1992, the head of the Catholic Church, Pope John Paul II, apologised for its condemnation of Galileo.

Creation versus evolution

In the nineteenth century, Darwin's ideas about evolution shocked people who had always believed that every type of creature was created by God. Today, as the sources on these two pages show, many people still discuss whether it is possible to agree with the theory of evolution and also believe in a creator God. As you read sources B and C, try to think why schools in the USA are not allowed to teach both the biblical and the scientific accounts of the origins of the universe.

3 What do you think of the news stories B and C? Why do you think the US Supreme Court made the decision in Source C? Do you think that pupils should be allowed to hear both sides – the religious and scientific accounts? Give reasons for your answer.

source B

Evolution theory removed from syllabus

The theory of evolution has been removed from what pupils in Kentucky, USA, are expected to learn. Teachers argue that this is wrong, because pupils need to be taught all ideas about the beginnings of the universe. They are concerned that some religious people are trying to stop discussion of this important issue.

7 October 1999

source C

Call for Bible teaching

Teachers and parents in West Virginia, USA, are arguing against a Supreme Court ruling from over ten years ago, which bans schools from teaching their pupils about the biblical creation story. The teachers and parents are calling for the right to teach the creation story as an alternative to evolution, so that pupils can see that there are different explanations.

17 December 1999

Sources D to H come from an on-line chat room where people discuss the relationship between religion and science. Think about which opinions are closest to your own. You will be using this information for an extended piece of writing.

source D

'We certainly believe in the intelligent design of the universe. We believe that the creation myth tells us more about who WE are and who GOD is and what our relationship with each other and with God should be, than it tells us anything about the literal HOW of creation.'

Rev. Gregory S. Neal, USA

source E

'Islam defines science as the best way to know God.'

Abdullah Ahmed, Jordan

source F

'I am a Christian and also a scientist. To me evolution is the way in which God created all the different animals in the world.'

James Herbst, USA

source G

'To me creation is obviously the work of God. Nothing this complicated could happen by accident or from a few fragments colliding together.'

Janice Johnson, New Zealand

source H

'No one ever claimed that the Christian religion is a science. It is not important whether God created the earth in seven days or whether each of these seven days is meant to represent billions of years. The fact is the earth is a magnificent system ... Many things just work and scientists still cannot always explain why. To our knowledge there is no other place in the universe with so much life. This in itself is already a miracle.'

Vivien Cooksley, Austria

4   Is it possible for a person to believe both in the Big Bang and in God? If so, what explanation of the beginning of the universe might this person give?

5   Some people consider religion and science to be quite different: religion is faith and science is a process of knowing. Others do not see such a clear distinction. Have a class discussion in which you answer some of the following questions:
- Are there issues of faith involved in modern science?
- Are there things that science does not know as fact?
- Is there any way that religion can be a means of acquiring knowledge?
- In what ways can you say that religious truth is a form of knowledge?

Write up your findings

As a conclusion to Unit 4, record your findings in an extended piece of writing. Use the question 'Are science and religion in conflict?' as your title. Before you start writing, think up the arguments you want to use.

● Make a list of statements you wish to use.

● Look through the material in Unit 4 and pick out pieces that may help your argument.

Use the following paragraph starters to help you structure your writing:

● Although not everybody would agree, I want to argue that ...

● I have a number of reasons for arguing this point of view. My first reason is ...

● Another reason is ...

● Lastly ...

● Therefore, although some people might argue that ...

● I think I have shown that ...

Questions about life ... and death

In Unit 5 we will explore what the religions say about some of the big questions in life. What makes a human being? What is the purpose of life? Why is there suffering? What happens to people when they die?

5.1

Who am I?

What is a human being? On the surface this may seem an easy question to answer, but the moment you start trying to give your answer, the harder it becomes. Different people answer the question in different ways. Scientists describe the human person in biological or chemical terms [A], whilst physical anthropologists concentrate on how humans are different from other creatures [B, page 58]. If you ask your relatives who you are, they may well say things like 'you're just like your mum'. Religions describe the human person in relationship to God [C to I, pages 58-59].

a person with roles and responsibilities

'A famous poet, John Donne, once said "no man is an island". He was exactly right. None of us exist by ourselves. We all are part of a greater whole. We all have roles and responsibilities within the local communities in which we live as well as in the world as a whole. We are all responsible for making the world a better place.'

a body and a soul

'I believe that I am more than my body. I have a mind and a soul. At death I will not just end. My soul will be reincarnated into another body. I also have a mind which can think and make decisions.'

source A

A human being is a mixture of chemicals

- iron enough to make one medium-sized nail
- magnesium enough for one dose of salts
- sulphur enough to rid one dog of fleas
- lime enough to whitewash a small building
- sugar enough for seven cups of tea
- fat enough for seven bars of soap.

a Sikh

'Sikhism has had a big influence upon my life. I have been brought up as a Sikh, and have inherited from my religious tradition many of my beliefs and values. I believe that all people are equal and should be treated as equals. I am also tolerant of other religious beliefs.'

the result of all the influences upon me

'I am who I am not just as a result of how I was born, but also because of the influences which people have had on me. In my early childhood I was greatly influenced by my parents, and shared many of their likes and dislikes. As I became a teenager my friends had a greater influence upon me. Today we are all influenced by the media, by television and magazines.'

my own personality

'There is no one exactly like me. I am unique, a one-off, a creature of God. I am my own crazy mix of thoughts and feelings.'

the product of a mixture of genes from my parents

'Each person inherits genes from their parents. I have often been told that I have my dad's personality. My genetic code, DNA, contains all the secrets about me – my gender, my looks, and even parts of my personality. Some people even say that genes affect other things, for example, intelligence, and sexual orientation.'

1 **a** Answer the question 'Who am I?' in as many ways as possible, beginning 'I am ...

   b Is the scientific description in source A (page 56) true? If so, in what sense is it true? What does this description miss out?

   c Write down any puzzling questions that you have about yourself and your relationships with others and the world.

2 No two people are exactly alike; even twins are different. In what ways are you different from anyone else?

source B

A new exhibit at Copenhagen Zoo

In 1996 the Copenhagen Zoo announced a new exhibit. A pair of Homo sapiens were put in a glass-walled cage. The zookeeper Peter Vestergaard said the exhibit would force people to 'confront their origins', causing them to accept that 'we are all primates'. After all, he added, humans and apes share 98.5 per cent of the same chromosomes. But look at the difference 1.5 per cent makes. In other cages their hairy neighbours were swinging on bars, whilst the two humans read books, checked email, sent faxes, and so on.

3 If we are 98.5 per cent like other animals, what makes humans different?

The Jewish and Christian views

In Judaism and Christianity every person is believed to be of unique value because humans are created in God's image. Each person's life has a purpose.

source C

'Beloved is Man because he was created in the image of God.'

The Talmud

source D

'Then God said, "And now we will make human beings; they will be like us and resemble us. They will have power over the fish, the birds, and all animals" ... So God created human beings, making them to be like himself. He created them male and female, blessed them and said, "Have many children".'

Genesis 1: 26-28

'Yahweh our Lord: how majestic is your name throughout the world!

I look up at your heavens, shaped by your fingers, at the moon and stars you set firm –

What are human beings that you spare a thought for them, or the child of Adam that you care for him?

Yet you have made him little less than a god, you have crowned him with glory and beauty,

made him lord of the works of your hands, put all things under his feet,

sheep and cattle, all of them, and even the wild beasts, birds in the sky, fish in the sea.'

Psalm 8

source F

'Man was first created as a single individual, to teach the lesson that whoever destroys one life is regarded by Scripture as if he destroyed the whole world. And Scripture regards whoever saves one life as though he saved the whole world.'

The Talmud

source G

'Aren't five sparrows sold for two pennies? Yet not one sparrow is forgotten by God. Even the hairs of your head have all been counted. So do not be afraid; you are worth much more than many sparrows!'

Luke 12: 6-7

source I

'Surely you know that you are God's temple and that God's Spirit lives in you!'

1 Corinthians 3: 16

source H

'You created my inmost self, knit me together in my mother's womb.'

Psalm 139: 13

4 **a** Use sources C to I to explain why Jews and Christians believe that each person is special.

b How do you think people's actions should be affected by the belief that they are created to be like God?

➤ *When a person has had a heart transplant, are they still the same person as before? What if it becomes possible to transplant brains? Would this change who the person is?*

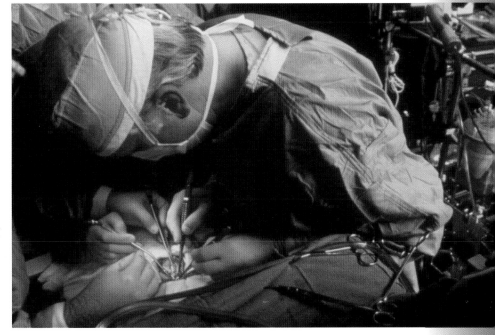

I AM THE SUM OF MY PARTS

The Buddhist view

The Buddha compared the human person to a cart. If you take the cart to pieces you end up with all its parts. But where would the original cart be? It would no longer exist. Only the separate parts would be left. It is much the same with the so-called 'person'. Buddhism teaches that there is no such thing as the self. This teaching is called *anatta*, which means 'no-self'. Instead, a human being is made up of five 'heaps'. When a person dies, all these five heaps break up. There is no actual thing called a self. We are just the coming together of these five heaps.

▼ *The five 'heaps' which make up a human being, according to Buddhism, are: (1) matter/the body; (2) feelings and sensations; (3) perception using our five senses; (4) the mind; and (5) consciousness.*

THE BODY   FEELINGS   SENSES   THE MIND   CONSCIOUSNESS

60

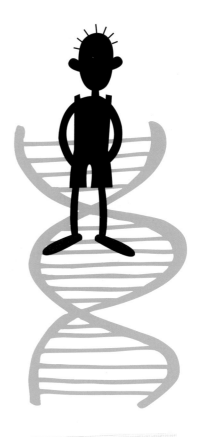

5 What was the Buddha saying about humans by comparing them to a cart? Do you think this is an accurate comparison? Is there any evidence to support the belief that each person has a self?

6 **a** Each one of us is unique, a 'one-off'. There are many things about us that make us unique, which other people do not see: our feelings and secret thoughts. By yourself, write down the four most important things about the 'real' you. These may be things that only you know. Ask yourself:

- What makes me very happy?

- What makes me annoyed?

- What do I like doing by myself?

- What do I think about most when I am alone?

b Now use these four things to write a poem using the title 'Who Am I?' If you wish, you could start your poem with the words 'When I looked in the mirror, what did I see …'.

7 How do you describe somebody? Split into groups. Choose one member of the group to write about. All members of the group should write their description of the chosen person, using only positive statements. Compare your descriptions. How are they the same? How are they different? Why do you think they differ? Is it possible to choose the most accurate description?

➤ *Here's what one student wrote, in answering question 6.*

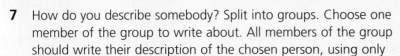

Who Am I?

We say 'I am me',
But who is me?
What are we really?
A lump of flesh, a mass of cells,
I'm not just some pencil lead and a lime!

I'm me, a living, breathing soul,
A lively spirit,
A creation of human life.
I have a lot to say for myself,
I'm not just iron and water.

I have feelings, sensitivity,
The ability to love, and be loved,
To feel hurt, but I can also harm others.
I'm not some complicated chemistry set,
This living spirit is me.
I AM ME!

(Abby, 13)

8 a What role do parents play in shaping who you are? To what extent are you like your parents? Do you look like them in any way? Do you share interests? Are you like your parents in personality? Draw a table with two columns. One column should be headed 'ALIKE', the other 'NOT ALIKE'. Fill in the table, listing how you are like and how you are not like your parents.

b To what extent do children copy their parents' behaviour? Do you think children who see their parents reading are more likely to enjoy reading? What about children who see their parents smoking? What about parents who play a musical instrument?

c Do you think children grow up to be different from their parents? In what ways are they different? What factors make them different?

◄ *Dad and Mum ...*

▼ *... and their son and daughter.*

9 Do magazines and television have an influence on you? How might television affect your tastes in clothes and food, or even your appearance?

10 Now think about who influences you most. Copy the chart below. In the second column, marked R for 'Ranking', number the people 1 to 9, with 1 being who influences you the most and 9 being who influences you the least. In the right-hand column explain how the people influence you.

Influences

Person/people	R	How they influence me
Friends		
Politicians		
The media (television, etc)		
Parents		
Brothers and/or sisters		
Religious people		
Teachers		
Pop stars		
Sports men and women		

What's life about?

Most of us lead busy lives. From the moment we wake up until the time we go to sleep we always seem to be doing something: going to school, eating, meeting friends, watching TV, doing homework. Our days fill up quickly. It's not surprising that we probably don't often stop still and ask what the purpose of all these activities is. We know why we have to eat, because our bodies need food in order to survive. But do we ever ask ourselves what the bigger purpose is?

1 Take a few minutes to write down your goals in life. What are you aiming for? What matters to you? Share these goals in a small group.

➤ *People's work often gives them a sense of purpose, especially if it is creative or involves caring for others.*

source A

Life's a game

'Life has often been compared to a game. We are never told the rules, unfortunately, not given any instructions about how to play. We simply begin at "Go" and make our way around the board, hoping we play it right. We don't exactly know the objective of playing, nor what it means to actually win. The Ten Rules for Being Human answer the fundamental question, "What is the purpose of life?" These are the guidelines to playing the game we call life ...

1. You will receive a body.
2. You will be presented with lessons.
3. There are no mistakes, only lessons.
4. Lessons are repeated until learned.
5. Learning does not end.
6. "There" is no better than "here".
7. Others are only mirrors of you.
8. What you make of your life is up to you.
9. All the answers lie inside of you.
10. You will forget all of this at birth.

(from C. Scott, *If Life is a Game, These are the Rules*, 1999)

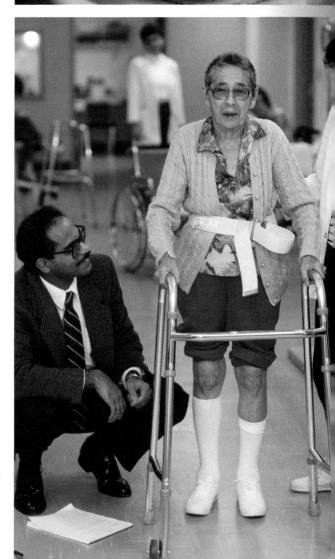

Life's about loving others and being loved in return. This is the most important thing.

As long as I am happy, that's all that's important.

WHAT'S LIFE ABOUT?

source B

Riding on a conveyor belt

'I feel that my life is like a conveyor belt which I can't get off. It's just one long meaningless line. I was born without anyone asking whether I wanted to be. I go to school, get a job to earn enough money to get married, have children, grow old, and then die. What's the point?'

HAVEN'T WE GOT TO TERMINAL 1 YET?

Life's about enjoying things. If we don't learn to celebrate life it's our own fault.

Life's about having loads of new and exciting experiences.

You've just got to get through life – sometimes it's tough, sometimes it's easy. There's no real meaning to life.

Born to reproduce and die

There is a type of insect that doesn't have a mouth. It is a species of moth with no obvious digestive system. When the adult moth emerges from the chrysalis it has no way of taking in food and starves to death within a few hours. The moth has been designed to reproduce – to lay eggs to pass on its life. Once it has done that it has no further reason for living, and so it is programmed to die. Are we like that? Or is there a meaning to life beyond simply existing and passing on our genes?

I'M HUNGRY

2 What's life about? What is *your* answer to this question?

People have different ideas about the point of life and describe life in various ways. Sometimes life is compared to a journey. Sometimes it is likened to a survival game – where the players try to stay in from the beginning to the end, dealing with obstacles along the way. Some people make their one aim in life to become very rich, or famous. Sadly, some people lose all sense of direction in life, and they may become ill [E].

Carl Jung (1875-1961), a famous psychiatrist, wrote:

'About a third of my cases are suffering from no clinically definable neurosis, but from the senselessness and emptiness of their lives.'

Carl Jung, *Modern Man in Search of a Soul*

Living for yourself never brings satisfaction. Only living for others does.

Darlink what's ze matter? We have it all.

It's all about fame and riches, or is it?

A young man left home when he was 18, in search of fame and fortune in America. He had three dreams when he set out – to make a million pounds, to drive a Porsche, and to marry a beauty contest winner. He took his chances in the computer technology business and by the time he was 35 he had accomplished all three. However, he had also become very depressed. Although he had accomplished his dream, his life had lost all meaning. He had run out of dreams, and he ended up feeling 'is this all that there is?'

The point of life and life to come – what the religions say

The religions of the world teach that life *does* have a purpose, and that there is something beyond a person's life and death in this world.

Buddhists, Hindus, and Sikhs believe in a cycle of birth, death, and rebirth: when a person dies, the soul is reborn into another life. How a person acts in their present life affects the sort of life they will be reborn into [F]. For people from these religions, the aim is to live responsibly so that they may achieve freedom from the cycle of birth, death, and rebirth. Many Hindus and Sikhs believe that achieving that freedom means being united with God.

Judaism, Christianity, and Islam teach that people have only one life on earth. People in these religions should live in such a way as to be able to have life after death with God.

Jewish scriptures tell Jews to enjoy the pleasant things in life and to see God in them [G]. They also include a story of King Munbaz, who gave away all his wealth to the poor during a period of famine. His relatives told him off, but he told them that by giving away his money, he was storing a different kind of treasure for the future [H].

source F

'A man who has been away on a long journey is welcomed with joy on his safe return by his family and friends. You should regard your present life on earth as a long journey; and if you are to accomplish this journey safely, you must devote yourself to good works. Then when you are born into your next life, you will be welcomed by all around you.'

The Dhammapada 220

source G

'In the world to come, each of us will be called to account for all the good things God put on earth which we refused to enjoy.'

The Talmud

source H

Munbaz answered his relatives, when they complained about his giving the family wealth to the poor:

'My ancestors stored up treasures for below, but I have stored treasures for above. They stored up treasures that yield no fruit, but mine will be productive. They stored up treasures of money, but I stored up treasures of souls. They stored up treasures for this world, but I for the World to Come.'

The Talmud

CHANGE FOR THE BETTER!

Christians believe that the purpose of life is to love and serve God [I]. Because Christians believe that God became a human person in Jesus, they also believe that one way of loving and serving God is to love and serve other people.

The Christian Bible likens life to a race, with the end goal being to live in oneness with God [J].

source I

The Catholic Catechism is a book of instruction used to teach people about their faith. It is written in question and answer form and starts with the words:

Question: Who made you?
Answer: God made me.

Question: Why did God make you?
Answer: God made me to know him, love him, and serve him in this world, and to be happy with him for ever in the next.

◄ *A Christian community centre. Running a centre like this is one way for a church to serve people in the local community.*

source J

'Run in such a way as to win the prize. Every athlete in training submits to strict discipline, in order to be crowned with a wreath that will not last; but we do it for one that will last forever.'

1 Corinthians 9: 24-25

3   Ask five people outside school to complete the sentence: 'My main purpose in life is ...'. As a class, collect all the responses and design a wall frieze with the title 'The Purpose of Life'.

4   Draw your own picture summing up what you think life is about. Give it a label.

5   'If death is the end, then life has no meaning.' Have a class debate about this statement. Split into two sides, one to argue that life has no point unless there is some kind of life after death, and the other to argue that life does have a point, even if there is no life after death.
Use the writing frame on the right to prepare your speeches for the debate.

- Although not everybody would agree with me, I want to argue ...

- I have several reasons for taking this point of view. My first reason is ....

- Another reason is ....

- My final reason is ....

- Therefore, although some people might argue that ....

- I think I have shown that ....

5.3

Why do we suffer?

If you watch the television news or look at a newspaper on any day, you are likely to see examples of the suffering that people endure. 'Why do we suffer?' is one of the hardest questions to answer fully. In Unit 5.3 we will consider a variety of forms of suffering, and find out how Christians and Buddhists explain and respond to suffering. You will have the opportunity to reflect personally on why suffering exists and what you can do to help people who are suffering.

1 In quietness, think of examples of suffering that you have seen in your life. It could be suffering that has happened to your family, or to your local community, or something that you have seen on the television. Write down these examples using the following headings to help you.

- I remember when …

- What I saw made me feel …

- I would like answers to the following questions.

▲ *This Russian child has breathing difficulties caused by air pollution from industry.*

◄ *Suicide.*

➤ *Escaping from floods in a Korean city.*

◄ *A patient in the intensive care unit of a modern hospital.*

▼ *These people are victims of landmines, used during civil war in Angola. Landmines are bombs laid near the surface of the ground, which explode when people walk over them.*

2 What is happening in each of these five pictures? Write a title for each one.

3 a Match each photograph to one of the following:
   - suffering caused by the person themselves
   - suffering caused by medical reasons
   - suffering caused by human beings
   - suffering caused by natural events beyond human control

  b Say whether humans – groups or individuals, caused the suffering in each photograph.

  c Was the suffering in the photographs avoidable?

4 Choose a news event that is an example of suffering and research it by using the search engine on one of the following news websites:
- www.telegraph.co.uk
- http://news.bbc.co.uk
- http://www.independent.co.uk/news

Then report back to the class, describing what form of suffering it is and what has caused it.

source A

Massacre at Dunblane School

A local man, 43-year-old Thomas Hamilton, walked into Dunblane school's gym yesterday and, without warning, opened fire on teacher Gwen Mayor and her class. In 3 to 4 minutes Mrs Mayor and 16 children were killed, and 17 other children and teachers wounded. Mrs Mayor died trying to shield her pupils. In a final act Hamilton turned the gun on himself and shot himself dead.

Dunblane, Scotland, 14 March 1996

Sometimes a horrible event happens which catches everyone's attention. In March 1996 attention focused on a tragedy that took place at a small school in Dunblane, Scotland [A].

source B

A telegram from the Pope said:
'The Holy Father ... invoke's Gods consolations upon all those suffering as a result of this senseless violence and he sends his blessing.'

▼ *The relatives of those who died dedicated a memorial garden to the sixteen children and their teacher.*

source C

'This garden is a beautiful place in which we can all remember the loved ones we lost.'

Mick North, whose daughter Sophie was killed

Why did it happen?

We can all learn from suffering – maybe Dunblane was something we could learn from.

If we always did what we felt like, other people would suffer.

If people were not allowed to have guns it wouldn't have happened.

We can all lose our temper.

We are all capable of doing horrible things.

We all have a choice to do right or wrong.

Hamilton lost control.

Everything happens for a reason, even when we don't know what the reason is.

One response to this tragedy was that the government made a law banning people from owning handguns.

Eight of the parents whose children died later launched the 'Dunblane Tartan Ribbon Appeal'. Money raised by selling the tartan ribbons is given to the Save the Children organisation. It is then used to help children suffering all over the world [D].

source D

One of the Dunblane parents, Liz McLennan, whose daughter Abigail was murdered, said: 'I lost my daughter and I felt that I would really want to help children all over the world, and in this country, who are suffering from crime and suffering generally.'

5   In source B, what did the Pope mean by 'this senseless violence'? Do you think that sometimes there is no sense or meaning in suffering?

6   Can good ever come out of suffering? What good things happened as a result of the Dunblane tragedy?

7   Who do you think was to blame for the tragedy at Dunblane? Consider each of the following possibilities:

   - Thomas Hamilton, who made a bad choice

   - society, which allowed Hamilton to own a handgun

   - Thomas Hamilton's parents, who have some responsibility for their son's values

   - the school, which didn't have enough security

   - anyone else?

Suffering and religion

Religions cannot ignore suffering. The existence of suffering raises some hard questions:

- Does God exist?
- If God does exist, why doesn't God do something about the suffering?
- What sort of God allows innocent people to suffer?
- Why do people suffer?
- Is there any purpose to suffering?

A positive side?

It is possible to think of examples of suffering being useful in some way or having some positive effects [E-H].

8 Carry out a survey of ten people, asking them why they think there is so much suffering in the world. Write up your findings under the title 'Reasons given for suffering'.

source E

'I am reminded of the story of Pinocchio. He is made of wood, so is insensitive to pain. But when he let his leg loll in the fireplace near his fire, his insensitivity to pain became a great danger and threatened his life. It seems absurd to say it, but: what would happen if there were no pain to sensitise us in time, to warn us? What would have stopped the junkie last night? What would warn the alcoholic of the disorder in which he lives?'

Roman Catholic, Brother Carlo Carretto

source F

Leprosy

Leprosy is a disease of the nervous system. It stops people feeling pain. The problem with this is that, when people don't feel pain, they also cannot sense when something is wrong with their body and get help for it.

source G

'Thank God for pain.'
Paul Brand, an expert on leprosy

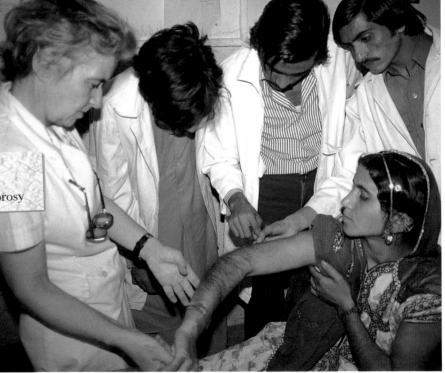

➤ *Doctors care for a leprosy patient in Karachi, Pakistan.*

◄ Villagers in Orissa, India, stand by their home which was destroyed by a typhoon.

source H

Typhoons

Countries such as Bangladesh and India are hurt by typhoons. However, when typhoons stay away, so does rain – and this would cause drought and more suffering.

Some of the greatest world leaders suffered much in their upbringing. For example, Alexander the Great, Julius Caesar, Napoleon, Lenin, Castro. Suffering does not need to destroy a person; what counts is how the person reacts to the suffering [I, J]. Suffering sometimes brings out positive qualities in people [K].

source I

'What doesn't destroy me makes me stronger.'
Martin Luther King Jr

source J

Abdul Baha of the Baha'i religion thinks that suffering helps people to form character:

'Those who suffer most attain to the greatest perfection ... People who do not suffer attain no perfection. The plant most pruned by the gardeners is the one which, when the summer comes, will have the most beautiful blossoms and the most abundant fruit.'

source K

This prayer was found scribbled on a piece of wrapping paper near the body of a dead child at a Nazi death camp in the Second World War:

'O, Lord, remember not only the men and women of good will, but also those of evil will.

But do not remember all the suffering they have inflicted upon us;

remember the fruits we have borne thanks to this suffering –

our comradeship, our loyalty, our humility, our courage, our generosity, the greatness of heart which has grown out of all this;

and when they come to the judgement, let all the fruits that we have borne be their forgiveness.'

The Holocaust

When the Nazis came to power in Germany in 1933, they began to pass many laws against Jews. They spread the idea that Jews were an 'inferior race' and should be exterminated. Between 1939 and 1945, during the Second World War, the Nazis killed over 6 million Jews in concentration camps and death camps. This persecution of Jews is sometimes called the Holocaust, a word that means 'burnt offering'. More than any other event in recent history, the Holocaust has caused Jews to ask the question, 'Why do innocent people have to suffer so?'

How has the suffering of the Jewish people affected their belief in God? In the 1970s one thousand survivors of the Nazi camps were interviewed. Almost half of them said that their suffering had not affected their belief in God. Five per cent of them actually said that they had started to believe in God as a result of their suffering.

▲ *These men were liberated from a Nazi concentration camp in Ebensee, Austria, on 7 May 1945.*

9 Using sources E to L, write a paragraph in which you explain whether suffering can sometimes be a good thing or whether it is always bad.

Christianity's view on suffering

Christians believe that God gave humans free will – the ability and freedom to choose between doing good and doing evil. As soon as humans were granted free will, human evil was let loose in the world, and it is human evil that causes a lot of the suffering that we see around us. Christians believe that people should take responsibility for this suffering.

The issue of suffering stands at the heart of Christianity. The religion is centred on Jesus, who Christians believe is the Son of God. Jesus lived a real human life and showed a special concern for people who suffered. He cared for people on the outside of society. For example, there are stories about Jesus showing love for people with leprosy; society normally shunned people with this disease. Jesus welcomed people to eat with him who were normally rejected by society in his time. The Bible also tells how Jesus performed miracles to heal the sick.

When Jesus was 33 years old, he suffered terribly himself as he was killed by being hanged on a cross. Christians believe that Jesus suffered on behalf of people. The cross is the main religious symbol for Christians. Because of Jesus' death on

▼ *For Christians, a cross is a symbol reminding them that Jesus, the Son of God, understands what it is like to suffer. Here, small crosses were laid on the ground by people campaigning for debt relief for the world's poor countries. The crosses were a way of saying that Jesus shares the suffering of starving children in the poor countries.*

▲ *The Resurrection, an icon by Sophie Hacker, in Cotgrave Church, Nottinghamshire. Why do you think Jesus' hands and feet still bear the marks of the Crucifixion?*

the cross, Christians believe that they are not alone when they suffer. God understands human pain and agony. In fact, God suffers with his creation [M].

Suffering is not the end of the story. The story of Jesus did not end with his death. After three days he was raised to life, and later returned to be with God in heaven. Christians believe that, when they die, they will also be raised to life. Being raised from death to life is called 'resurrection'. The last book of the Bible describes a time in the future when there will be no more pain and suffering [N].

10 Explain why the cross is the central symbol of Christianity.

source M

'Even if I go through the deepest darkness, I will not be afraid, Lord, for you are with me.'

Psalm 23: 4

source N

'He [God] will wipe away all tears from their eyes. There will be no more death, no more grief or crying or pain.'

Revelation 21: 4

Christians believe that in heaven there will be no more suffering. But does this mean that the suffering that people experience in this present world doesn't matter? This question was put very well by the Christian Russian writer Dostoevsky (1821-81) in his novel *The Brothers Karamazov* [O].

source O

The Brothers Karamazov

Two brothers, Ivan and Alyosha, both believe in God. Alyosha is training to be a monk. But Ivan is rebelling against God for making the world full of suffering. He says he cannot understand why the world is arranged as it is, and why innocent children suffer. He tells Alyosha about an eight-year-old boy who was punished for accidentally hurting the paw of his master's favourite dog:

'He was taken from his mother and kept shut up all night. Early that morning the general comes out on horseback, with the hounds ... The child is brought from the lock-up. It's a gloomy, cold, foggy autumn day for hunting. The general orders the child to be undressed; the child is stripped naked. He shivers, numb with terror, not daring to cry ... "Make him run," commands the general. "Run! Run!" shout the dog-boys. The boy runs ... "At him!" yells the general, and he sets the whole pack of hounds on the child. The hounds catch him and tear him to pieces before his mother's eyes! ...

'I don't want the mother to embrace the oppressor who threw her son to the dogs. She dare not forgive him! ... the sufferings of her tortured child she has no right to forgive. Is there in the whole world a being who would have the right to forgive and could forgive? ... too high a price is asked for harmony; it's beyond our means to pay so much to enter. And so I hasten to give back my entrance ticket. And that I am doing. It's not God that I don't accept, Alyosha, only I most respectfully return Him the ticket.'

'That's rebellion,' murmured Alyosha, looking down ...
'Tell me yourself, I challenge you – answer. Imagine that you are creating a fabric of human destiny with the object of making men happy in the end, giving them peace and rest at last, but that it was essential and inevitable to torture to death only one tiny creature ... would you consent to the architect on those conditions?'

11 Are there any conditions under which the general should be forgiven? Who do you think has the right to forgive? Are certain crimes unforgivable?

12 How do you think Alyosha answered Ivan's question at the end of this passage? How would *you* answer it? Do you think some suffering is necessary for the ultimate good?

13 In what way does Ivan challenge Alyosha's belief in God? What questions do you think he would like to ask God, if he could meet him?

World Vision – helping those who suffer

Each religion has organisations that give practical help to people who are suffering. In 1950 Dr Bob Pierce founded the Christian organisation World Vision, to help orphaned children in Asia. Today World Vision is the world's largest Christian international relief and development agency. It works in over 88 countries, giving help to all in need, whatever their religion or race. It helps communities with water programmes, health care, education, agricultural and economic development, and Christian leadership.

source P

World Vision's Mission Statement

'World Vision is an international partnership of Christians whose mission is to follow our Lord and Saviour Jesus Christ in working with the poor and oppressed to promote human transformation, seek justice and bear witness to the good news of the Kingdom of God.'

World Vision seeks to follow the example of Jesus:

- in his love for the poor and those who are on the outside of society
- in his special concern for children
- in the respect he showed for women
- in his call to share things equally between people
- in his love for all people, whatever their colour of skin or race
- in his offer of new life through faith in him.

▲ *Dr Bob Pierce had a vision of a world without hunger, disease, and hopelessness. In its first 50 years, the organisation he founded helped over 50 million people.*

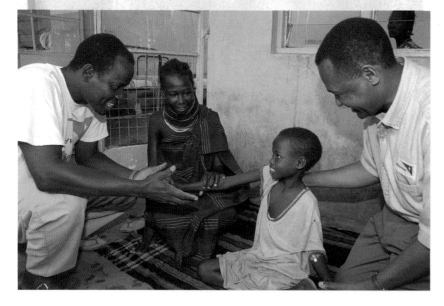

source Q

'We encourage people to sponsor children in poor communities so that they can be given a God-given hope for a better future. Today over 1.9 million children are helped in this way.'

World Vision

source R

Serving the poorest of the poor

On 13 January 2001, El Salvador was hit by a massive earthquake. Before the earthquake, nearly 50 per cent of the population already lived in poverty. In the earthquake, more than 1,200 people were killed, 5,000 injured, and 1.5 million made homeless. World Vision provided food, shelter, and medicine to 3,000 families with immediate needs. It also helped local people to build affordable housing.

source S

Encouraging peace in Kosovo

In the 1990s Kosovo was torn apart by ethnic war. Today World Vision is building the first multi-ethnic school in Kosovo since the end of the war. It is called 'a project of peace'.

14 Imagine that you are a television producer sent to make a TV documentary about World Vision. The documentary should describe the work of World Vision and also explain the central Christian beliefs that motivate the organisation's work. Visit the World Vision website on www.wvi.org to collect more information and find out about current projects. Write a plan of your documentary, explaining the type of photographs you would use and including some example script to go with them.

Buddhism's view on suffering

15 How do you 'see' life? Complete the sentence, 'Life is ...'.

Buddhism starts from the observation that all existence, including human existence, is imperfect in a very deep way. 'Suffering I teach – and the way out of suffering,' said the Buddha. The Buddha is sometimes compared to a doctor who diagnoses the suffering of the world and then offers a cure. In his first sermon the Buddha summed up his diagnosis in the Four Noble Truths.

The Four Noble Truths

1. Dukkha (suffering, or unsatisfactoriness) is part of everyday life

The Buddha observed what happened in the world and, like a doctor, identified the 'disease' in life. Instead of running smoothly, life is filled with the miseries of unhappiness, sickness, old age, and death. The reason for our unhappiness is that we find it difficult to accept that things in life are always changing. For example, if I am happy spending time with a friend, I am unhappy when my friend has to leave. People who have every material thing in the world spend their life protecting what they have because they are afraid of losing it.

The nature of life is that it is full of changes – and so unhappiness or suffering is a part of life. The Buddha called this suffering *dukkha*. It is a word that suggests restlessness and unsatisfactoriness.

2. Suffering is caused by craving

The Buddha then identified the cause of *dukkha*. He taught that we experience *dukkha* because we are always craving or 'thirsting' for other things. Some people show this attitude to material things: they are always wanting the latest thing to buy. What they have is never good enough. They always want more.

3. Dukkha can be ended

If the cause of *dukkha* is thirsting or craving, the end of *dukkha* is obvious – stop craving and thirsting [T].

4. The cure of suffering

The Buddha then gave people the prescription for their cure. He taught that people can practise letting go of craving by following certain moral and spiritual disciplines. He summed these up in the Noble Eightfold Path.

source T

'Not in great wealth is there contentment, nor in sensual pleasure, gross or refined. But in the extinction of craving is joy to be found by a disciple of the Buddha.'

The Dhammapada 186-7

---

16 Look through today's newspaper and pick out stories that support the view that life is unsatisfactory. Choose one of these stories to share with the class.

17 Look through the photographs in this unit so far. Do they support the view that life is unsatisfactory and full of suffering?

18 a Advertising is always encouraging you to buy things because they will make you happy. Make up a collage of adverts. What are they advertising? What do they think will make you happy?

b What things have you really wanted in life? Did you get these things? Did they make you happy? If so, how long did the feelings of happiness last?

19 Design a poster with the title 'Is life unsatisfactory?' First decide whether you agree with the Buddhist point of view. Then choose images to include. What quotes could you use?

The Noble Eightfold Path

The Noble Eightfold Path, prescribed by the Fourth Noble Truth, sums up the Buddha's teaching about how to end craving [U]. The Buddha compared his teaching to a raft on the sea of life. Sometimes life is stormy, at other times it is calm. People need the raft to take them across the sea of life.

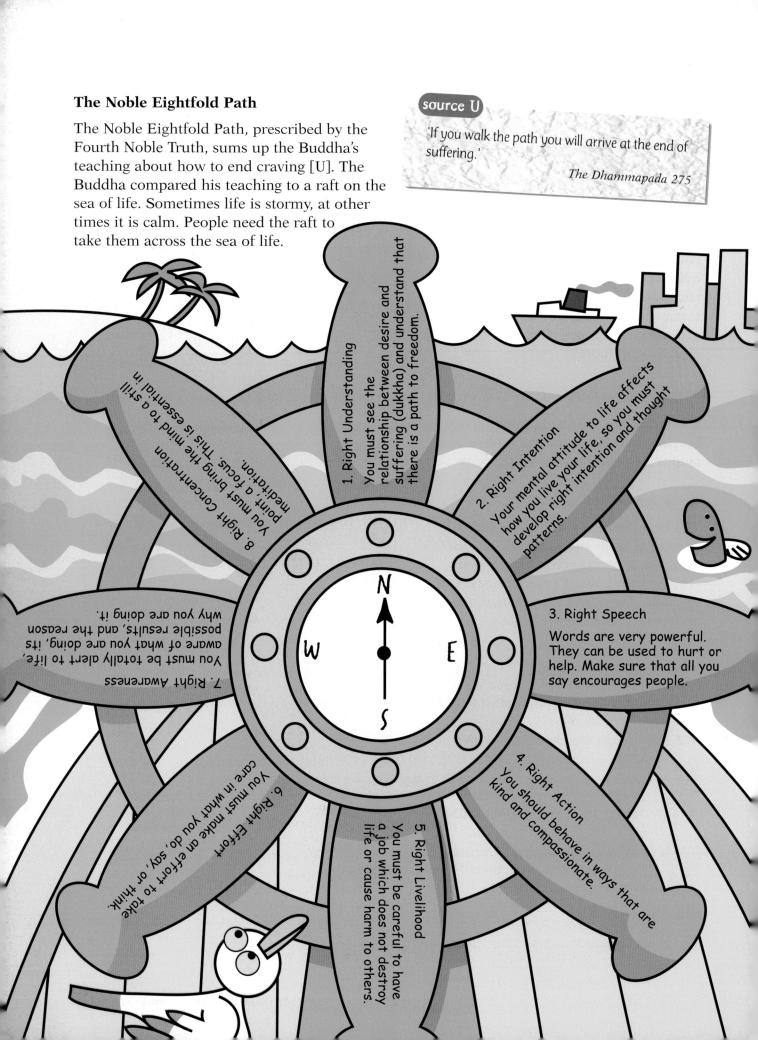

1. Right Understanding
You must see the relationship between desire and suffering (dukkha) and understand that there is a path to freedom.

2. Right Intention
Your mental attitude to life affects how you live your life, so you must develop right intention and thought patterns.

3. Right Speech
Words are very powerful. They can be used to hurt or help. Make sure that all you say encourages people.

4. Right Action
You should behave in ways that are kind and compassionate.

5. Right Livelihood
You must be careful to have a job which does not destroy life or cause harm to others.

6. Right Effort
You must make an effort to take care in what you do, say, or think.

7. Right Awareness
You must be totally alert to life, its aware of what you are doing, its possible results, and the reason why you are doing it.

8. Right Concentration
You must bring the mind to a still point, a focus. This is essential in meditation.

20 If the sea stands for human life, what events in life might be represented by (a) a rough sea and (b) a calm sea?

21 Draw the Noble Eightfold Path, as a wheel with eight spokes. Label each of the eight paths. By each spoke, either draw a sketch or write an example of what you think each path means.

Right Attitude

Following the path of Right Intention means having the right attitude to life. How does a person's attitude affect the way they suffer? Michael [V] is an example of someone who approached his suffering with a great attitude.

I FEEL **TWICE** AS GOOD TODAY!

source V

'It's your choice how you live life'

Michael is the kind of guy you love to love. He is always in a good mood and always has something positive to say. When someone would ask him how he was doing, he would reply, 'If I were any better, I would be twins!' He was a natural motivator. If an employee was having a bad day, Michael was there telling the employee how to look on the positive side of the situation.

... One day I went up to Michael and asked him, 'I don't get it! You can't be a positive person all of the time. How do you do it?' Michael replied, 'Each morning I wake up and say to myself, you have two choices today. You can choose to be in a good mood or you can choose to be in a bad mood. I choose to be in a good mood. Each time something bad happens, I can choose to be a victim or I can choose to learn from it.'

'Yeah, right, it's not that easy,' I protested.

'Yes, it is,' Michael said. 'Life is all about choices. You choose how you react to situations. You choose how people affect your mood. You choose to be in a good mood or bad mood. The bottom line: It's your choice how you live life.'

Soon after that I lost touch with Michael as we both moved jobs. Several years later, I heard that Michael was involved in a serious accident, falling some 60 feet from a communications tower. After 18 hours of surgery and weeks of intensive care, Michael was released from the hospital with rods placed in his back. I saw Michael about six months after the accident. When I asked him how he was, he replied, 'If I were any better, I'd be twins. Wanna see my scars?' I asked him what had gone through his mind as the accident took place.

'The first thing that went through my mind was the well-being of my soon to be born daughter,' Michael replied. 'Then, as I lay on the ground, I remembered that I had two choices: I could choose to live or I could choose to die. I chose to live.' ...

Michael continued, '...the paramedics were great. They kept telling me I was going to be fine. But when they wheeled me into the ER and I saw the expressions on the faces of the doctors and nurses, I got really scared. In their eyes, I read "he's a dead man". I knew I needed to take action.'

'What did you do?' I asked.

'Well there was a big burly nurse shouting questions at me,' said Michael. 'She asked if I was allergic to anything. "Yes", I replied. The doctors and nurses stopped working as they waited for my reply. I took a deep breath and yelled, "Gravity!" Over their laughter, I told them, "I am choosing to live. Operate on me as if I am alive, not dead."'

Michael lived, thanks to the skill of his doctors, but also because of his amazing attitude. I learned from him that every day we have the choice to live fully. Attitude, after all, is everything.

(from R. D'Ausilio, *Wake Up Your Call Center*)

22 a Do you ever get into a bad mood? What causes you to do so?

b What does it feel like to be in a good mood?

c Give an example of how your attitude can change the way you see life.

23 Do you think Buddhists would think that Michael had a right attitude? What was his attitude to suffering? Do you think it is possible for all people to have this attitude?

24 a What is happening in the illustration on the right? What might have caused this situation? What forms of suffering are taking place? Make sure you include feelings as well as thoughts.

b Now apply the teachings of the Eightfold Path to the situation. What might the people learn from the Eightfold Path?

25 Write up your answer to the question: How do Buddhists believe that suffering can be overcome?

Where do we go when we die?

1 What do you think happens to you when you die?
2 Read the following opinions. Pick out the one that is closest to your own view and explain why.

Some opinions on death and life after death

Death is a subject I try not to think about.

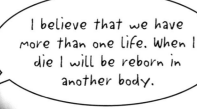

I believe that we have more than one life. When I die I will be reborn in another body.

I feel that sleep and dreams must have something to do with death.

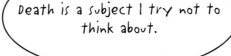

Funerals should not be unhappy times. I wouldn't want people wearing black at my funeral.

Jokes about death cover up our fear.

I believe in life after death. I believe I will go to heaven.

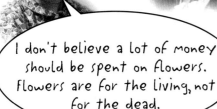

I don't believe a lot of money should be spent on flowers. Flowers are for the living, not for the dead.

When you die you should let your body be used for medical research and for saving lives.

NOW WHAT'S GOING ON?!

source A

Death is like birth

Imagine birth from the viewpoint of the foetus in the womb. Your world is dark yet secure. You do nothing for yourself. Life is just a matter of waiting – you're not sure what for, but any change seems scary. Then one day you feel a tug. The walls seem to press in. Those soft padded walls are pushing you downwards. Your body is bent double. For the first time in your life you feel pain. There is more pressure, almost too intense to bear. Your head is squeezed flat and you're pushed harder into a dark tunnel. You hear a groaning sound and you are filled with fear. Your world is collapsing. You suddenly see a light at the end of the tunnel. You are held upside down and slapped. You have just been born.

Death is like that. From this side of life it seems scary. It's like being sucked along a dark tunnel, pressure all around you. You are full of fear – fear of the unknown. But beyond the darkness and the pain lies a whole new world outside. When we awaken after death in the bright new world, the tears, hurt, and pain will be a mere thing of the past.

Christianity: life after death

Christians believe that Jesus came back to life after he had been killed on the cross. This rising from the dead is called the Resurrection. The Bible contains accounts of Jesus' followers going to the tomb where Jesus had been buried and finding it empty. There are also accounts of times when the disciples met with the risen Jesus. Christians believe that because Jesus 'conquered death' and rose to new life, they also have the promise of being raised to new life after death [B].

source B

'Jesus said: "I am the resurrection and the life. He who believes in me will live, even though he dies; and whoever lives and believes in me will never die."

John 11: 25-26

source C

Jesus told his followers: 'Do not be worried and upset. Believe in God and believe also in me. There are many rooms in my Father's house, and I am going to prepare a place for you.'

John 14: 1-2

3 Imagine that you have the opportunity to interview God. List five questions that you would like to ask God about the end of human life. Discuss these in small groups. Are any questions the same? If so, why do you think this might be?

4 Read sources C to F. What do you learn from these Bible quotes about what Christians believe about life after death?

source D

'This is how it will be when the dead are raised to life. When the body is buried, it is mortal; when raised, it will be immortal. When buried it is ugly and weak; when raised, it will be beautiful and strong. When buried, it is a physical body; when raised, it will be a spiritual body.'

1 Corinthians 15: 42-44

source E

In the last book of the Bible the new heaven is described: 'God himself will be with them, and He will be their God. He will wipe away all tears from their eyes. There will be no more death, no more grief or crying or pain.'

Revelation 21: 3-4

source F

'We shall not die but ... we shall be changed in an instant, as quickly as the blinking of an eye ... The dead will be raised, never again to die and we shall all be changed. For what is mortal must be changed into what is immortal.'

1 Corinthians 15: 51-53

▲ *This is a picture of a family meeting in heaven, as imagined by the British poet and artist William Blake (1757-1827).*

Heaven and hell

Some Christians believe that a life that completely ignores God will result in punishment in hell [G].

source G

'Do not be afraid of those who kill the body but cannot kill the soul; rather be afraid of God, who can destroy both body and soul in hell.'

Matthew 10: 28

5 What pictures come to mind when you think of (a) heaven, and (b) hell? What colours are in each of your pictures?

The Bible describes hell in a very pictorial way [H]. Some Christians believe that everything written in the Bible is true – and so they believe that hell is a fiery place of punishment. Others find it difficult to believe in hell as well as in the Christian God of Love. In source I, a character from a novel – a priest called Father Nicholas – explains what he thinks about hell, and the kind of judge God is.

source H

'Whoever did not have his name written in the book of the living was thrown into the lake of fire.'

Revelation 20: 15

source I

What kind of judge is God?

'I doubt if Jesus would have favoured these scenes of torment which show a Grand Inquisitor tossing people into the flames. Jesus seems to have been more interested in speaking about a shepherd who went out of his way to search for a lost sheep – and that brings me to the story I wanted to tell you about the sheepdog trials.

'You know what I mean by sheepdog trials, don't you? They're open-air exhibitions of the skills dogs show when herding sheep, and the judge has to decide which dog is the most skilful. Well, once upon a time, a man and his small son were on holiday in the Lake District and they saw a sign to some sheepdog trials. The little boy said: "Oh, I'd like to see a trial!"

'But when they arrived the little boy was very disappointed. He said: "But where's the jury? And where's the judge in the black cap, like the judge at the Old Bailey who sentences murderers?"

'His father had to explain that it wasn't that kind of trial. No dog was going to be condemned to death or sentenced to prison. Every one of them was there to be valued and encouraged, and if some didn't come up to the mark they were always told they were welcome to come back later when they had learned how to be more skilful ...

'God is like the judge of the sheepdog trials, not like the judge in the black cap at the Old Bailey ... because nothing in the end can separate us from the love of God, nothing, of that I'm quite sure.'

(abridged version, from S. Howatch, *The High Flyer*, 1999)

6   **a** What does source I tell us about (i) Jesus, (ii) judgement, (iii) God?

    b How do sources H and I differ in their description of judgement and punishment?

A new life

The story of 'Water bugs and dragonflies' [J] explores what happens after death. It talks about a new life. Christians believe that, in their new life, they will be given a new spiritual body and will be with God.

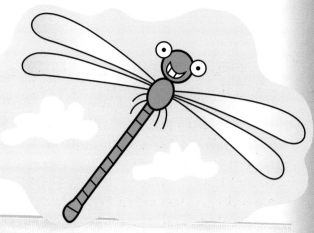

7 Write your own story explaining Christian ideas about life after death. Bring out the following ideas which are present in source J:

- there is a change
- there is a new existence
- there's no going back
- those who are left behind can't understand it, and they make up their own explanations.

8 In what ways does the story of the water bugs and dragonflies help you understand the Christian belief in resurrection?

source J

Water bugs and dragonflies

At the bottom of the pond there lived a colony of water bugs. For most of the year they played happily. But every now and then one of the water bugs would stop playing with them. It would climb up a lily stem and disappear from their sight. It never returned. Where had it gone? The rest of the water bugs were puzzled. They came up with a number of explanations. Some thought there was a bug eater which gobbled up bugs when they reached the surface. Others thought that when a bug got to the top, that was the end – it just disappeared into thin air. That must be the end of its existence, or it would have come back and told them what had happened.

One of the water bugs then had a plan. The next time a bug climbed up a lily, it would promise to come back and tell the rest where it had gone to and why.

Not long after, the water bug that had come up with this plan found itself climbing up a lily. Before it knew what had happened, it had climbed so far that it popped through the surface of the water into the brilliant sunshine. As it looked around it noticed the most amazing thing. Its body had changed. It now had four beautiful wings. As the sun dried off its body it fluttered the wings and miraculously found itself flying above the water. It was so exciting, soaring through the air.

By chance it came to land on a lily pad. As it looked into the water it saw the colony of water bugs it had left behind. Suddenly it remembered its promise to return and tried to swoop down into the water. But as soon as it hit the water it bounced back. It could no longer return. 'I can't keep my promise', it cried. 'All I can do is to wait for my friends to follow me. Then they will understand.' The dragonfly soared up into the beautiful air.

(Retelling of original story 'Water bugs and Dragonflies', by Doris Stickney)

ONLY US TWO LEFT!

9 What do you think happens after death? Do you believe in a life after death? If so, what do you believe?

10 What long-term goals do you have in life? Do these include your views about the afterlife?

Hinduism: belief in reincarnation

We can follow the cycle of life in nature. Many things seem dead in winter, but each spring they are recreated. They develop and grow during the summer, then decay in the autumn, and die. The cycle never stops.

Human beings are born, they live, they may reproduce, and they die. Hindus believe that, at death, the soul passes into another body. The soul is the real self, called *atman*. In this way the soul passes from one body to another, throughout the various species of life. This is called reincarnation.

Hindus believe that the soul takes its next body according to the law of *karma*. This is a moral law which holds that each soul is totally responsible for its own actions. So a person's present condition is the result of the way they lived in their previous lives; and their actions now determine their future states of being. However, Hindus are taught not to judge people who are suffering.

source K

'As a man acts, as he behaves, so does he become. Whoso does good, becomes good; whoso does evil, becomes evil.'

Brihadaranyaka Upanishad

90

11 Think of an example to show that actions have natural and often foreseeable consequences. As a class, role-play some of your examples.

12 a What is meant by 'whoso does good, becomes good; whoso does evil, becomes evil' (source K)? Provide examples from life to illustrate this saying.

  b Do you agree that good actions lead to wisdom, happiness, and freedom, whereas bad actions lead to misery and ignorance?

13 If something good happens to us, do we take credit for it? How do we react if something bad happens to us? Is it possible that acts of kindness or evil actions come back to us? Why are we not all born equal? Why is one person born into luxurious circumstances and another born blind and deaf? What are some of the advantages of the law of *karma*? What may make the law of *karma* difficult to accept?

This diagram shows how some key Hindu beliefs relate to each other. The cycle of birth, death, and rebirth continues many times. The ultimate goal for Hindus is to escape this cycle by achieving liberation (*moksha*), when they are reunited with God (Brahman). Hindus are taught that there are a number of ways to connect to God. The most important are *karma yoga* (the way of selfless action), *jnana yoga* (the way of spiritual knowledge), and *bhakti yoga* (the way of loving devotion).

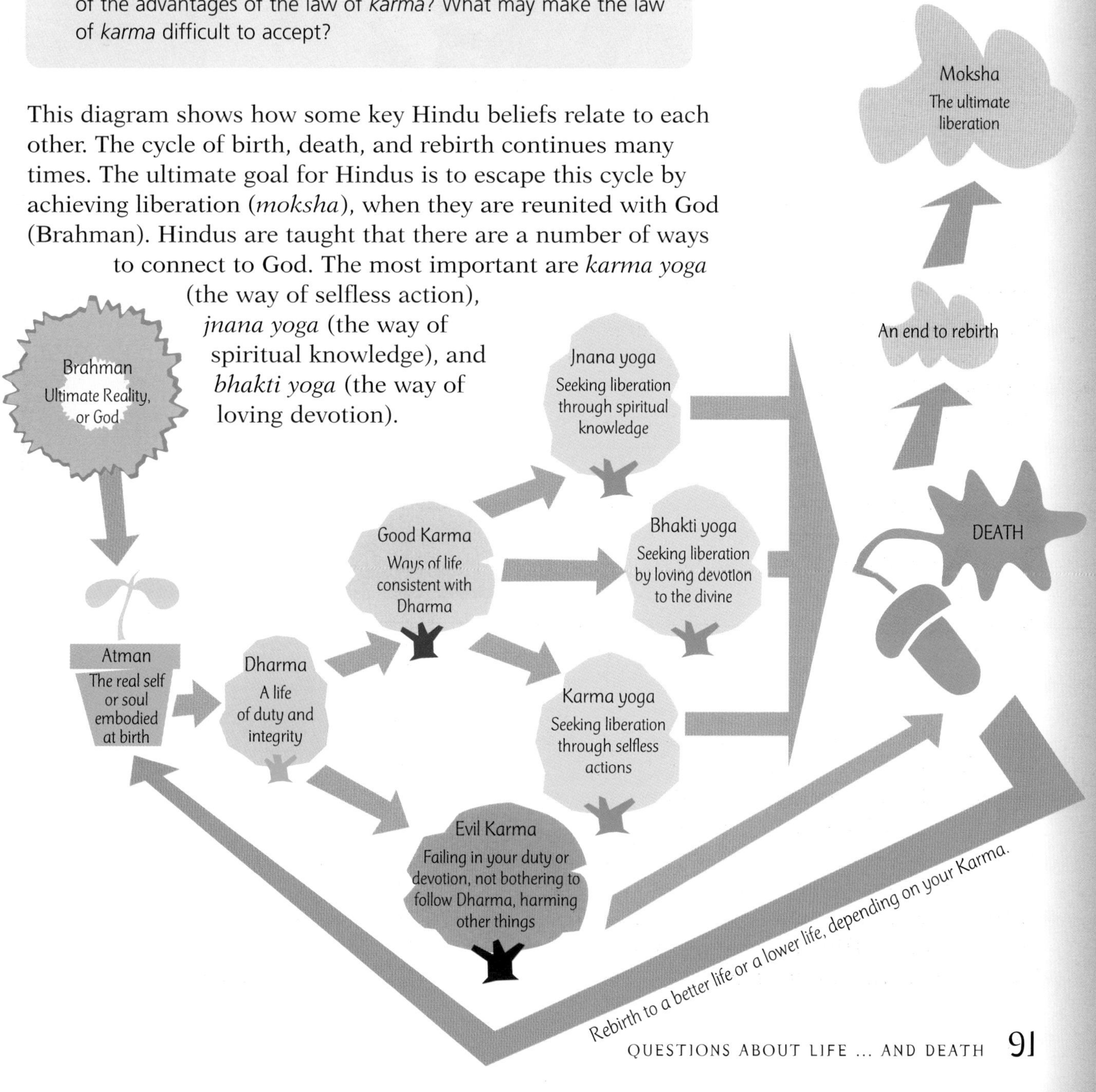

Moksha
The ultimate liberation

An end to rebirth

Jnana yoga
Seeking liberation through spiritual knowledge

Bhakti yoga
Seeking liberation by loving devotion to the divine

DEATH

Brahman
Ultimate Reality, or God

Good Karma
Ways of life consistent with Dharma

Karma yoga
Seeking liberation through selfless actions

Atman
The real self or soul embodied at birth

Dharma
A life of duty and integrity

Evil Karma
Failing in your duty or devotion, not bothering to follow Dharma, harming other things

Rebirth to a better life or a lower life, depending on your Karma.

14 Make a glossary of key words related to belief in reincarnation.

15 Study the diagram about the Hindu cycle of life on page 91. Then produce your own chart to show the cycle, illustrating each part of it with drawings and magazine cut-outs of faces, people, and activities.

16 Suggest two ways in which belief in reincarnation may affect how a Hindu lives their life. Share these ideas with the class.

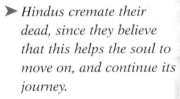

➤ *Hindus cremate their dead, since they believe that this helps the soul to move on, and continue its journey.*

17 Look at the views on page 93. What reasons are given
(a) in favour, and
(b) against, the belief in reincarnation?

18 Which of the statements are closest to your own view? Explain why.

17 Look at the views on page 93.

> **source L**
>
> 'As a man abandons his worn out clothes and acquires new ones, so when the body is worn out, a new one is acquired by the self, who lives within. The self cannot be pierced or burned, made wet or dry. It is everlasting and infinite, standing on the motionless foundation of eternity. It is beyond all thought, all change. Knowing this you should not grieve.'
>
> *Bhagavad Gita 2: 22, 24-25*

Do you believe in reincarnation?

'The belief of reincarnation is another method of persuading people to behave well in this world.'
(Stephanie)

'Under hypnosis people have provided accounts of their previous lives.'
(Maddy)

'Reincarnation is a good idea because it means that good will be rewarded and evil punished. It's fair and just. However, it's just a fantasy. Instead of looking for future karmic justice, we should try to make this world a better place here and now.'
(Nasser)

'I don't believe in an afterlife. The only chance is here and now. It's our world cup everyday. We mustn't waste this life.'
(Mark)

'Everything in the universe is recycled. It is therefore quite possible that there is that electro-magnetic force called the soul which is recycled to work out misdeeds.'
(David)

'Without reincarnation the world wouldn't be fair.'
(Denis)

'Yes, because I have met small kids who know exactly who they were in previous lives.'
(Matesha)

'I hope not because I'll be coming back as a worm in my next life for all the wrong I have done.'
(Matthew)

Write up your findings

As a conclusion to Unit 5, record your findings in an extended piece of writing. Use the question 'Where do we go when we die?' as your title. Use the following paragraph starters to help you structure your piece of work:

● Before I began this topic I thought that ...

● When I read about different religious beliefs I found out that Christians believe ...

● The reasons Christians believe this are ... (use a quotation from Christian scriptures to support what you say)

● I learned that Hindus believe ...

● The reasons Hindus believe this are ... (use a quotation from Hindu scriptures to support what you say)

● It was interesting that ...

● My conclusion, based on this evidence, is ...

Sacred books quoted in the sources

Bhagavad Gita

This is the most important scripture for many Hindus. It was written between 200 BCE and 200 CE. It tells the story of Krishna as an *avatar* of Vishnu, coming to earth in human form to teach people how to overcome evil and lead dutiful lives.

Brihadaranyaka Upanishad

The *Upanishads* are Hindu scriptures written down between 400 and 200 BCE. There are 108 of them. They are records of discussions led by teachers called *gurus*.

Corinthians

Corinthians is found in the New Testament, part of the Christian Bible. It is a letter written by St Paul in around 54-55 CE to the church in Corinth that he had founded. Paul wrote the letter to answer major questions that the church was asking.

Dhammapada

The *Dhammapada* is part of the *Sutta Pitaka*, a collection of the sayings and discourses of the Buddha. It consists of 423 verses on morality and mental discipline. It was probably compiled in the third century BCE.

Genesis

Genesis is the first book of the Jewish Bible and of the Christian Old Testament (the first part of the Christian Bible). It tells of the beginning of the world and contains stories about the first man and woman. The second part of *Genesis* (chapters 12-50) is a history of the origins of the Hebrew nation.

Gospels of Matthew, Luke, and John

The Gospels are the first four books of the New Testament (the second part of the Christian Bible). They are accounts of the life, teaching, death, and resurrection of Jesus Christ. The Gospels of *Matthew* and *Luke* are generally held to have been written between 70 and 80 CE.

Christian Church tradition says that the Gospel of *John* was written by St John the Evangelist and published late in the first century, possibly in the ancient Greek city of Ephesus.

Guru Granth Sahib

The *Guru Granth Sahib* is the main sacred text of Sikhism. Sikhs believe that it contains the Divine Word (*Gurbani*), which came to the Sikh Gurus direct from God.

Mool Mantra

This is the basic statement of Sikh belief at the beginning of the *Guru Granth Sahib*.

Psalm

The book of *Psalms* is part of the Jewish Bible and the Old Testament of the Christian Bible. It is a collection of 150 hymns and poems. Seventy-four of the psalms are said to have been written by King David, and twelve by his son and successor, Solomon.

Qur'an

The *Qur'an* is the main sacred text of Islam, containing what Muslims believe are the revelations made by Allah to the Prophet Muhammad. It is divided into 114 chapters called *surahs*.

Revelation

Revelation is the last book of the Christian Bible. Tradition says that it was written by St John, the author of the fourth Gospel. It was written to give hope to Christians facing persecution in the Roman Empire. It would give them faith in life after death.

Talmud

The *Talmud* is a collection of Jewish civil and religious law. *Talmud* is a Hebrew word meaning 'instruction'. The *Talmud* is made up of a codification of laws, called the *Mishnah*, and a commentary on the *Mishnah*, called the *Gemara*.

Acknowledgements

Photographs

The Author and Publishers thank the following for permission to use the photographs in this book:

Bridgeman Art Library: pages 15t (Private Collection), 21t (Private Collection), 32 (Keble College, Oxford), 41 (Private Collection; Phillips, The International Fine Art Auctioneers), 76 (Cotgrave Church, Nottinghamshire, UK); Camera Press: pages 13b, 14br, 29r, 34, 51, 69t, 75; Circa Photo Library: pages 33b, 37 (John Smith); Corbis Images: pages 4 (Joseph Sohm; ChromoSohm Inc.), 5b (David H. Wells), 6b (Kevin R. Morris), 7t (Dave Bartruff), 11l (Suki Coe; Eye Ubiquitous), 11r (Raymond Gehman), 19b (Arvind Garg), 27t (Joe McDonald), 27b, 29l (Earl and Nazima Kowall), 31 (Kevin R. Morris), 33t (David Lees), 42t (Judy Griesedieck), 46 (Roger Ressmeyer), 53 (Bettmann), 63t (Kevin R. Morris), 63b (David H. Wells), 74 (Bettman), 87 (Historical Picture Archive); Christine Osborne Pictures: pages 5t, 6t, 6c, 18, 67, 72, 92; Panos Pictures: pages 13t (Howard Davies), 68t (Heidi Bradner), 73 (Piers Benatar); Popperfoto/Reuters: pages 14t, 14bl, 24b, 70; Science Photo Library: pages 22-23 (Jerry Schad), 24t (Stephen and Donna O'Meara), 42b (Bill Bachman), 44 (Space Telescope Science Institute/NASA), 47 (Dr Jeremy Burgess), 49 (Michael W. Tweedie), 59 (Alexander Tsiaras), 68 (CC Studios), 90 (John Heseltine); Still Pictures: pages 7b (Robert Mulder), 8b (Mike Kolloffel), 23 (Luiz C. Marigo), 69c (Mike Schroder), 69b (Hartmut); TRIP/H. Rogers: page 19t; World Vision: pages 78, 79.

Quotations

Scriptures on pages 20, 22, 58, 59 (E and H) quoted from *The Jerusalem Bible*, published and copyright © 1966, 1967, and 1968 by Darton, Longman and Todd Ltd, and Doubleday, a division of Random House Inc, are reproduced by permission of the publishers.

Scriptures on pages 59 (G and I), 67, 76, 86 and 87 quoted from the *Good News Bible*, published by The Bible Societies/HarperCollins Publishers Ltd, UK, copyright © American Bible Society, 1966, 1971, 1976, 1992.

Extract from Dostoevsky's *The Brothers Karamazov* from the translation by Constance Garnett in *The Gospel in Dostoevsky: Selections from his Works* (Plough Publishing House, 1988), copyright © 1988 by The Plough Publishing House of the Bruderhof Foundation, reprinted by permission of the publishers.

Extract from Rosanne D'Ausilio: *Wake Up Your Call Center: How to be a Better Call Center Agent*, reproduced by permission of the publisher, Purdue University Press.

Extract from Susan Howatch, *The High Flyer* (Little Brown & Company, 1999), reprinted by permission of the publishers.

Extracts from World Vision website at www.wvi.org, reproduced by permission of World Vision International.

Further details of other publications quoted in this book are as follows:

Shirley du Boulay, *Voice of the Voiceless*, Hodder and Stoughton, 1988

Cherie Carter-Scott, *If Life is a Game, These are the Rules*, Broadway Books, New York, 1999

Bishop Richard Harries, *Questioning Belief*, SPCK, 1995

Susan Howatch, *The High Flyer* (Little Brown & Company, 1999), reprinted by permission of the publishers

Michael Poole, *Science and Belief*, Lion, 1990

We have tried to trace and contact copyright holders before publication but have not been able to do so in every case. If notified, the publishers will be pleased to rectify any errors or omissions at the earliest opportunity.

Websites

Oxford University Press accepts no responsibility for material published on websites referred to in the book. Website addresses included were correct at time of going to press, but beware that these may change.

Index